Positive strategies for managing
and preventing out-of-control behavior

NO MORE
MELTDOWNS

JED BAKER, Ph.D.

FUTURE HORIZONS INC.
Arlington, TX

All marketing and publishing rights
guaranteed to and reserved by:

FUTURE HORIZONS INC.

721 W. Abram Street
Arlington, TX 76013
Toll-free: 800-489-0727
Phone: 817-277-0727
Fax: 817-277-2270
Website: *www.FHautism.com*
E-mail: *info@FHautism.com*

Printed in the United States of America

Cover and interior design © TLC Graphics, www.TLCGraphics.com
Cover: Tamara Dever; Interior: Erin Stark

ISBN 13: 978-1-932565-62-1

ACKNOWLEDGMENTS

I am most grateful to my clients and my own children who, through their honesty and openness, have taught me all of the lessons described in this book.

In addition, several individuals offered their valuable suggestions to create the finished product. My long time friend, Steven Amsterdam, an accomplished writer himself, generously edited several renditions of the manuscript. My wife, a talented therapist and writer, reviewed the work whenever I asked and put up with my own meltdowns. Carol Kranowitz not only graciously agreed to write the foreword, but she also helped me come up with the title of the book one evening after we did a presentation together.

My thanks must also go to Wayne Gilpin, president of Future Horizons, who took a chance to support me on a different kind of book. And last, but not least, Kelly Gilpin, who, under insane deadlines, had to turn the manuscript into a real book, with final edits, an awesome cover, and layout.

TABLE OF CONTENTS

The Problem
Chapter 1

What is a meltdown?
The usual parenting advice: start with rules and consequences
The limits of discipline: when rewards and punishments no longer work
But aren't meltdowns just manipulative behavior?
Can we really expect no more meltdowns?
An overview of the four-step model for reducing meltdowns

Chapter 2

Fight, flight or freeze response
Temperament
Difficulties with abstract thinking and perspective taking
Inflexibility
An explosive combination

The Solution
Chapter 3

Controlling our own frustration
Building competence

Chapter 8

Just wait
You can't always get what you want
Okay, time to stop playing

Chapter 9

Winning isn't everything
It's okay to make mistakes
But names will never hurt you

Chapter 10

I can't play with you now
Don't be jealous
Time to go to bed

Chapter 11

Prevention plan form

FOREWORD

by Carol Kranowitz, M.A.,
author of *The Out-of-Sync Child*

An ancient Greek myth tells the story of Sisyphus, a king who continually enrages, frustrates, and defies his family, his royal subjects, his guests, and his gods. Always he must push everyone around so he comes out on top. Never will he listen to reason, use good judgment, or obey the gods. His faulty behavior escalates until he pushes the gods beyond their patience, and they decide to teach him a lesson. The punishment is that for all eternity he must shove a huge boulder up a hill. With great effort, he can push the stone to the top where it hovers for a nanosecond and then, maddeningly, topples down to the bottom. Forever, he is doomed to chase after the boulder, put his shoulder to it, and push it up the hill again.

And again, and again.

In your home or classroom, do you know someone like this mythical king? Someone who frustrates or angers you with a contrary response to an ordinary demand (get out of bed, take just one bite of the carrot, keep your hands to yourself)? And does this person lack the skills to change his behavior? And do you try to cajole or reason with him, to no avail? Do the two of you get stuck in this no-win situation? Does the situation end with his inevitable meltdown and your futile punishment?

Or, do you feel like Sisyphus? When your interactions with your child give no satisfaction, you may be the one who seems always to be pushing a heavy "boulder," pointlessly and forever. You may feel unable to change the same-old, same-old cycle.

Do you wish someone would help you and your child break this cycle, so you could both get to the top—and stay there?

Okay, then! This book is for you!

Jed Baker, in this excellent book, gives us the tools to deal with and prevent out-of-control behavior. Wisely, he leads us grown-ups to understand how to change our own behavior in order to help our children change theirs.

Dr. Baker teaches through example, and these are compelling stories, indeed.

Perhaps you know a child like Kevin. Kevin misinterprets and lashes out at his classmates when they say he must wait to join a game. He gets more upset when grown-ups explain that his perception of the other kids' intent is inaccurate. He gets so upset that he has a meltdown.

Jeff avoids doing first-grade homework. He takes an hour to do a five-minute assignment and leads his parents on a chase through the house before collapsing in a meltdown.

Sandy eats only Goldfish crackers. She goes a whole day without eating if her parents withhold the crackers. At the end of the day, at the end of her endurance, and at the end of her parents' rope, Sandy has a meltdown.

Jared moves slowly in the morning. His parents' cajoling and raised voices result in his moving even more slowly. They push, he resists, and then (no surprise!), he has a meltdown.

Sound familiar?

A four-step program can prevent these incessant meltdowns—and make life so much easier! The first step is to accept and appreciate your child. Three "musts" in this first step are to control your own temper, create an atmosphere where the child feels competent, and avoid constant power struggles.

The second step is to de-escalate a meltdown with a distraction that you are pretty sure will comfort the child. The distraction may be a hug or a moment of bouncing on your knee. Physical contact and playful movement deliver soothing sensory input that may be all you need to diffuse the meltdown. If a hug or bounce won't do the job, the distraction may be a favorite toy, a good joke, or a collectible playing card.

The third step is to understand why meltdowns reoccur. You will learn the "ABCs" of behavior—Antecedent, Behavior, and Consequence—and determine the specific triggers of your child's meltdown.

The fourth step is creating logical plans to prevent meltdowns. These plans make so much sense that you will wonder why you didn't try them sooner. For instance, some children have meltdowns because they are on sensory overload—or "underload." Here you will find suggestions for ways to change the level of sensory stimulation that may contribute to out-of-control behavior.

You will learn to create a plan to alter the specific triggers to your youngster's meltdowns. This proactive approach explains how to teach new skills to prepare children for challenging situations. For example, Kevin learned through this approach to wait to join a game without getting upset, when he understood that his classmates were not rejecting him when they said he needed to wait.

I have a very high opinion of this book. It talks sense. It includes engaging case studies of recognizable children. It includes humor, especially when Dr. Baker reveals how his initial approaches to clients have occasionally backfired. It encourages us to become mindful, flexible, and hopeful, so we can model positive behavior for our children. Most of all, it is filled with compassion for the young "rulers" who reign over our homes and classrooms. These children are doing everything in their power to cope. Dr. Baker assures us that they can and will do so much better when their parents and teachers put their shoulder to the task, using the strategies suggested here.

CAROL S. KRANOWITZ, M.A.
Bethesda, Maryland
March 2008

INTRODUCTION

Like many therapists, I was steered into my profession by my upbringing. Emotional expression reigned supreme in my childhood. Not only did I receive my daily dose of love and appreciation, but I was also surrounded by plenty of anxiety, frustration and emotional outbursts. In many ways I have spent a lifetime trying to tune in and manage other people's emotions. Without knowing it, I learned to remain calm in a storm, using humor and distraction and any other means to pacify upsets.

I started my career as a psychologist at an inner city school system working with children referred for challenging behavior problems. Again I was called upon to put out "emotional fires" as my young clients frequently reeled out of control in their classrooms.

In my nine years there, I learned some crucial lessons that have stayed with me. First, I came to understand how vital it is to develop a trusting relationship. So many adults had failed these kids previously, it was no wonder that they had very little trust in me or any other professional hired to help them with their behavior. It was clear that I had to earn their respect before I could have any influence on them. I had to help them feel cared for and appreciated before they were willing to care about themselves.

A second lesson came out of frustration with my work in that setting. I grew tired of constantly putting out the same fires over and over again. It seemed that I was able to calm the students when they were upset, yet they continued to have the same problems time and time again. I needed a way to prevent these meltdowns rather than continue to simply calm the situation after the fact.

At this time I began working with students who had autism spectrum disorders. We were beginning to see more and more autism in the schools, especially in intelligent youngsters who had great difficulty adapting to the academic and social challenges of school. The autism literature was different from the literature available on working with my "emotionally disturbed" kids. Somehow, the autism researchers understood that kids with autism did not have the skills to cope with some of the academic and social challenges. Thus we needed to alter the demands placed on the children and teach them skills to cope with those challenges. The literature on kids with emotional disturbances erroneously assumed that those kids often knew how to behave, but just did not want to, and thus a "disciplinarian approach" was advocated.

No doubt discipline is an important part of working with all children. But I came to understand an important reality that extends beyond simplistic discipline: When children's problem behavior persists despite rules and consequences, it often means that they do not have the skills to cope with challenging situations. We must either change those situations or teach better coping skills.

As I continued my work teaching students on the autism spectrum how to deal with challenges, I began to write down the lessons I taught them. These grew into four books on social skills training (Baker, 2001; 2003; 2005; 2006). It became clear that the approach of modifying challenging situations and teaching coping skills was helpful, not only to autistic individuals, but to all children. I was eventually hired by another school district to oversee social skills training for all their students, where I've been able to see how these strategies have prevented many a meltdown.

Of course, all those years of professional work could not completely prepare me for having my own kids. As a psychologist, I usually have a quiet time to reflect on each of my client's needs. As a parent, I have to respond to my children's behavior in the middle of the night, first thing in the morning before coffee, and out in public. I have to calm my children, teach them skills, modify demands and love them as completely as I do—all while trying to live my life. It is my own kids, more than anyone else, who inspired me to write this book to provide parents with a brief reference guide to help us understand and manage some of the more challenging moments with our children.

Drawing on techniques from years of applied research on motivating children and managing challenging behavior, this book provides the tools to help us:

+ Accept and appreciate our children so that we can maintain a positive relationship with them.

+ Know how to calm our children so we won't feel helpless when their behavior is escalating out of control.

+ Create prevention plans for repeat problems so we can avert future meltdowns.

THE PROBLEM

1

MELTDOWNS:
When Rewards and Punishments are Not Enough

What is a Meltdown?

The family of a first-grader came to see me with concerns about their son. He had a challenging Kindergarten year. The school described him as a bright young boy with unpredictable outbursts. I met with his mother alone to get the background information on him. She explained how kind he was, yet misunderstood by those at school. The next week Mom brought him in to see me.

He entered the waiting room with a Game Boy in hand. I said with a cheerful tone, "Hi Chris, it's so good to meet you." He would not look up at me or respond, just continued with his Game Boy. I knew from his history that he could hear me. I tried to win him over, "Chris, what's that? A Game Boy? Can I see?" No response again. I said, "Can we talk for just a moment, you can bring your Game Boy in with you." No response.

I turned to Mom and asked what she usually does when this happens. She said, out loud, that she might take the Game Boy away. I said, trying to be positive, "Wait, don't do that. Chris, why don't you just bring the Game Boy in with you." He then put his fingers in his ears as I spoke and said, "Na, na, na, na," ignoring me.

I felt pretty powerless, much as I had the night before with my own kids when they ignored my efforts to get them to bed. This did not feel good. I began to wonder if it might be easier to work with adults, and let the rest of my staff work with the younger kids. Nevertheless, I tried one more thing, I took off my shoe, put a pencil up my nose and spoke into the shoe, "Chris, hello Chris, are you there?" I saw him smile. Without a word he followed me into my office.

I knew we were not home free yet, given our shaky start. I decided to quickly implement a little reward program to get him in a good mood. Mom told me he loved chocolate so I told him, "Every time you talk with me I am going to give you one of these fake dollars, and when you get five of them, you can have any of the chocolates in my bag over there." I began by asking him non-threatening questions like what his Dad's name was, his brothers', etc. Within a minute he earned five of the fake dollars. I said, "Look how many you have: 1, 2, 3, 4, 5. Go ahead—you can have any of the chocolates you like." At this point he squinted his eyes with an angry look, crawled under my desk, kicked over my chair, and began to knock his elbow into the drywall of my office hard enough to put a hole through it. He would not respond to me as he began to destroy my office.

This was a full-blown meltdown, the same kind seen in school as he began first grade. Did this young boy just need some firmer discipline? Was this a remnant of lack of discipline at home or in school? It seemed from the history that both school and home had offered rewards and doled out punishments to this boy fairly consistently. His mother's threats of more punishment after the session certainly had not calmed him down. A series of embarrassing hula dances I performed was enough to get him to laugh once more and calm down, yet the question remained: why did this happen, and would it happen again?

Mom clued me in to what might have happened. He was struggling in school with adding numbers and, as much as I thought I was rewarding him when I said, "look how many dollars you have," he thought, "This guy is doing math," prompting him to try to fight or flee from this threat.

These challenging moments are exhausting for all. They may involve any upsetting behaviors that are hard to control, such as kicking and screaming, refusing to listen, physical aggression, or bad language. From my point of view:

"Meltdowns" are escalating
negative emotional reactions.

The Usual Parenting Advice: Start with Consistent Rules and Consequences

Most good parenting books tell us that we need to create rules and be consistent in enforcing them. According to this straightforward advice, we need to control our own tempers and calmly follow through with the rules that we ourselves set if we want our children to behave. Not only is it difficult to stay calm in the face of meltdowns, but following through with rules and consequences is not always enough, as we will soon examine. However, creating rules and consequences is an important starting point, and the advice bears repeating here.

Most of us understand that kids need structure and discipline to help them learn and behave. We set rules so they know what is expected. We have consequences, both rewards and punishments, to make clear the importance of following those rules. Without rules and consequences, our lives would be chaotic.

One family I worked with complained about the difficulty they had getting their two kids to eat dinner with them at the dinner table. After some discussion, they acknowledged that their rules about eating dinner had been unclear and inconsistent for some time. If the husband and wife were tired after working late, they sometimes gave in and let the kids eat in front of the TV. Then, when they wanted everyone to eat together, it became a battle to get them to the table. With some coaxing, they agreed to make eating together at the table a consistent rule. The positive consequence of following the rule was some TV time later. If the kids violated the rule, there was no TV later. This consistency brought order to their home after two days, during which the children tested the new rule. A triumph for good old structure and discipline.

The Limits of Discipline, When Rewards and Punishments No Longer Work

Sometimes, when our rules are not being followed, we intensify our disciplinary efforts by handing out still more consequences. Let's look again at Chris, our first grader. He refused to do his work in class one day. The teacher told him he could not go to recess unless he did his work. He got angry and threw over his chair. She then said he must go to the principal's office and he responded by stating he hated her. The principal reprimanded him for his behaviors and said he would not be allowed to go to recess for two days. Chris became so upset, he tried to leave the school building. As a result, he was suspended. When he returned to school, he once again began to refuse to do his work and the cycle started over.

As another example, a seven-year-old child I worked with had trouble sitting at the table throughout dinner and would frequently get up, sometimes play with his food and, on occasion, throw food. His parents told him that following the rules to stay seated and eat his food would result in a favored dessert and TV time, but even after losing TV and dessert, the upsetting behavior would continue. Throwing food would result in being sent to *time out*. Upon returning from *time out*, the pattern would begin again, and then back to *time out* he would go for a longer time. When he did it a third time, his parents would take one of his favored toys. None of this seemed to alter his behavior. It certainly added stress to the family's life and left his parents questioning each other's discipline styles.

This kind of power struggle and escalation in discipline is fine if it leads to a positive change in behavior. But when it does not, it serves no purpose to continue in the same vein. All too often I hear adults in these situations say that the child is just spoiled, or that he or she just needs a firm hand.

When consistent rewards and punishments are not working, it is time to try a new strategy.

But Aren't Meltdowns Just Manipulative Behavior?

Some people distinguish between meltdowns and tantrums, suggesting meltdowns are always out of control while tantrums may be manipulative behaviors that are intentional. Returning to the example of Chris, who melted down in my office and at school, we might wonder whether his behavior was within his control. Did he plan to "act out" with me so that he would not have to go to therapy? Did he put on purposeful tantrums in school to get sent out of class because he did not want to do the work, or were these emotional reactions that overcame him when frustrated?

The issue of intent is often seen as crucial when considering whether or not to punish someone. If we think it's a manipulative act, we feel more confident following through with the enforcement of the rule. "You will do your work or lose recess!" If on the other hand we think the behavior is an uncontrollable emotional reaction, we might be more likely to give in: "Okay, let's take a break from work right now." Holding firm to rules or giving in are not our only choices. The third choice is to understand the problem so that we can create a plan to prevent it from happening. For Chris, that plan may involve altering the work so that he does not need to avoid it.

When the challenging behaviors continue despite consistently enforcing rules, it does not matter anymore whether the behavior was intentional. We need to understand how to alter the triggers to those behaviors and/or teach better ways to cope with those triggers.

That is what this book is about. When traditional discipline (using rewards and punishments) has fallen short, you need to know what to do. Chances are, if you are reading this book, it is because some challenging behaviors continue to happen despite your efforts. This book gives you the tools to: (1) Accept and appreciate your children, even when they are driving you crazy, (2) Calm a meltdown in the moment, and (3) Develop strategies to prevent future meltdowns.

Can We Really Expect No More Meltdowns?

If we could control the world, we could guarantee no more meltdowns. No longer would kids be asked to do things that are beyond their capacity. No longer would they have to wait too long for what they want. No longer would they be overwhelmed by noise or other over-stimulating events. We could make sure we had adequate time to prepare for challenging situations. We could control germs and sleep so that there would be no more illness or overtiredness, and ensure that our kids would be in the best possible shape to deal with the stresses of the day. Since we cannot control everything, *we will have meltdowns*. However, with understanding about what causes a meltdown, we can have fewer and fewer of these moments and reduce the stress in our own lives. The

8

following pages outline a four-step model for managing and preventing meltdowns and other behavioral outbursts. The model is based on research into the causes of such outbursts and evidence-based techniques to reduce such challenging moments.

An Overview of the Four-Step Model

Step 1: Accepting and appreciating your child

Two parents can react in the same way to a child's behavior, but one parent may be more likely to get the child to behave than the other because of their recent positive relationship. Many times in a school system, I have had administrators say to me that they cannot discipline certain children and must leave it up to another staff member whom the child trusts.

Maintaining a positive relationship is very much about managing our expectations and perceptions of our child. We must appreciate who the child is rather than try to force him to meet an unrealistic expectation. For example, a parent recently reported giving her one-year-old baby a "time out" because she was rocking too much in her chair and babbling too loudly. This is what one-year-olds do; trying to get a one-year-old to be perfectly quiet and not move is not a realistic expectation. Efforts to enforce rules that are not appropriate to your child can break down the relationship between child and adult and create more stress. When children feel accepted and appreciated by us, they are more likely to listen to us.

Chapter 3 describes the following key ways we manage our expectations to maintain a healthy relationship with our children:

1. First, we must be able to control our own temper. This is easier when we do not see the child's behavior as a threat to our own competence, but rather as a function of the child's current inability to cope with frustration.

2. Second, to reduce the child's frustration, we must create an atmosphere in which the child feels competent. If the child always feels criticized, he or she will begin to tune us out in an effort to protect self-esteem. Ample praise and setting up activities in which they can

succeed help to build a sense of competence and trust in the adult caregiver.

3. Finally, we must avoid constant power struggles. When children fail to follow a particular rule consistently, it may be time to change the demand rather than force them to comply. All children are different, thus the exact same expectations may not apply to all children.

Step 2: De-escalating a Meltdown

Because the world is unpredictable, we will not be able to plan for everything and there will be moments when our children melt down. We might take our kids to a toy store to get their friend a birthday present. We did not think to prepare them for the fact that we would not be buying them a present, too. Then our children see something they want and are told they cannot have it. Now comes the screaming and tantrum in public. People are staring and we feel judged and embarrassed, which makes us even more irritated, so we raise our voices at our kids—which escalates the situation even further. Now we have a real scene. We could just walk out, dragging our kids behind us. But is there a less stressful way to handle this?

What tools do we have to de-escalate this kind of situation? How can we manage an unexpected emotional meltdown? In Chapter 4, we will look at the art of distraction to de-escalate a meltdown that we were unable to prevent. Although this is a crucial crisis management skill, we do not want to rely on it too often. It would be much more productive to learn how to anticipate the situations that can trigger meltdowns and develop a plan to prevent them from happening. That is what Step 3 is all about.

Step 3: Understanding Why a Meltdown Keeps Occurring

When a child continues to have meltdowns, we must begin to reflect on why this is happening. We must assess if there is something predictable about the challenging behavior, if certain types of events tend to trigger them, and if the ways that others react enable the problem. Understanding why a meltdown occurs is key to developing plans to prevent them. Once we see a pattern emerging, and can predict meltdowns, we can begin to develop strategies to prevent them.

Chapter 5 lays out a method for assessing why we keep having the same meltdowns in certain situations. This process has an official name in the behavioral literature: Functional Behavioral Assessment.

Step 4: Creating Plans to Prevent Meltdowns

Once we understand why a meltdown occurs in a particular situation, we can create a plan to prevent it. Chapter 6 describes the components of a good prevention plan, which typically involves four areas of intervention:

+ Changes to the situations that trigger meltdowns.

+ Teaching skills to deal with the triggering situations.

+ Using rewards or losses.

+ Biologically based strategies.

Chapter Summary

+ All children need discipline; clear rules and consequences create order in our lives.

+ When rules and consistent consequences are not working to alter behavior, and meltdowns continue, we need to reflect on why the meltdowns occur.

+ A four-step model for managing and preventing meltdowns involves:

1. Managing our own expectations of our children so we can:

   – Control our temper
   – Create a sense of competence in our children
   – Avoid constant power struggles

2. Learning strategies to calm a meltdown in the moment.

3. Understanding why a meltdown occurs.
4. Creating plans to prevent future meltdowns.

2

WHAT ARE MELTDOWNS MADE OF?

Meltdowns are not abnormal behaviors. At a certain age, everyone has meltdowns. Self-control is something that develops with age, such that toddlers and preschoolers lacking in self-control are expected to have some meltdowns. Yet there are characteristics that make certain individuals more likely to melt down than their peers.

Meltdowns as the Fight, Flight, or Freeze Response

When we feel extremely threatened, we are all prone to react automatically with an intense emotional response to fight, flee, or freeze as if our life depended on it. This survival mode response in many ways fits the definition of a meltdown. Daniel Goleman, in his book titled *Emotional Intelligence*, refers to these moments as a state of being "hijacked by emotions" (Goleman, 1995). It is as if the emotion center has taken over the rest of the brain so that we don't have easy access to our reasoning ability.

Some people refer to this as the "crocodile" or "reptilian" brain taking over. The human brain has both the remnants of the old reptilian brain (particularly the limbic system), which controls the "fight-or-flight response" and the newer, human part of our brain called the neo-cortex, which is associated with planning and reasoning ability. When threatened, our reptilian brain may cause us to flee, fight, or freeze without the cerebral cortex intervening (i.e., without our ability to reason or think about what we are doing). This quick, non-thinking response certainly has survival value, but in a world where perceived threats may not always be life threatening, the fight, flight, or freeze response can lead to unnecessary meltdowns, causing us to automatically become upset when a cool mind might have been more effective.

Goleman (1995) points to the difficulties of trying to reason with someone during an emotional hijacking, and describes how distraction can shift the individual's attention away from the triggering event until she is calm. I will return to the issue of distraction in Chapter 4: De-escalating a meltdown.

An Overactive Emotion Center

Although anyone can have a meltdown, certain chacracteristics may be associated with an unregulated limbic system, leading to more difficulty controlling emotions. These include a difficult temperment, attention deficit hyperactivity disorder (ADHD), chronic pain, and sleep difficulties. All these are associated with greater irritability and emotional reactivity. We will look at the research on temperamental differences momentarily.

Characteristics That Make the Environment More Threatening

In addition to being more emotionally reactive, certain difficulties can make it more likely to feel threatened by what many would see as harmless events. Sensory challenges (e.g., sensitivity to noise, light, touch, smell, and taste) or difficulties integrating all these sensory inputs, as in sensory processing disorder, can make seemingly innocuous events feel like a threat to one's survival (see Kranowitz, 2006, for more on sensory processing disorders). Motor difficulties, especially speech problems, also make it more likely to feel threatened as it becomes difficult to communicate one's needs. Similarly, difficulties with abstract thinking, perspective taking and inflexibility can make unexpected events feel like major threats to one's integrity. Without the cognitive flexibility to understand and process new or challenging events, many individuals will be thrown into meltdown mode.

In the next sections we will examine in more detail how certain temperamental differences, problems with abstract thinking, perspective taking, and inflexibility can increase the potential for meltdowns.

Temperament

Long-term studies from infancy through childhood show that certain individuals are born with a more difficult temperament—one that is associated with greater negative emotional reactions to new situations, including tantrums or meltdowns when frustrated. Thomas and Chess (1977), in their now-famous studies of newborns, examined nine key dimensions of behavior:

1. Activity level
2. Rhythmicity (e.g., schedule of feeding, sleep, and elimination)
3. Approach/withdrawal patterns
4. Adaptability
5. Threshold of responsiveness
6. Intensity of reaction
7. Quality of mood
8. Distractibility
9. Attention span and persistence

Based on these nine dimensions, they were able to characterize about 60% of children into one of three categories and show that these patterns of behavior were often quite stable over time. The first category is the "easy child" who can accept frustration with less fussiness, maintain a more positive mood, and easily adapt to change. The second is the "difficult child" who shows a more negative response to new situations and more intense crying and tantrums when frustrated. The last is the "slow-to-warm-up child" who initially shows a mild negative reaction to new situations, yet gradually adapts with more exposure to those situations.

Both the "difficult child" and "slow-to-warm-up child" are more likely to be prone to meltdowns. And although these patterns seem to be stable characteristics over time, parental response can alter a child's temperament. For example, work by Kagan (1992) shows that timid youngsters who are gently encouraged to be more outgoing by their parents—and thus are gradually exposed to new situations—become less fearful.

Although having a difficult temperament does not mean one has a "behavior disorder," certain behavior disorders are associated with greater levels of frustration. Children with attention deficit hyperactivity disorder (ADHD) and some mood disorders such as bipolar disorder may have greater impulsivity and are less able to control their emotional reactions. In addition, those with autism spectrum disorders, sensory processing disorder, and anxiety disorders such as obsessive compulsive disorder may have greater challenges in handling new situations and prefer repetitive routines. We will now examine how problems with abstract thinking, perspective taking, and inflexibility also lead to difficulty handling unexpected events.

Difficulties with Abstract Thinking and Perspective Taking

What is abstract thinking? It is the ability to imagine that which is not directly perceived by the senses.

Take, for example, an interaction I once had with a bright teenager who did well academically, yet had difficulty at times relating to others—especially taking other people's point of view. I said to the boy, "Imagine that dogs could fly." He said, "Dogs can't fly." I repeated, "But imagine that they could." He reiterated, "No, they can't fly." When I said, "Imagine they had wings and they could fly," he began to get angry with me, insisting that dogs do not have wings and cannot fly.

This scenario was hard for the boy to imagine because it did not exist; there are no flying dogs. To imagine it, the part of your brain that has knowledge of dogs must interact with the part of the brain that knows about flying creatures to construct the abstract notion of a flying dog. Despite his good intellectual ability, he had trouble imagining abstract concepts. In school he excelled at rote memory tasks and had a vast amount of factual knowledge, yet struggled to understand imaginary, abstract concepts.

When one has challenges with abstract thinking, it may be difficult to take another's perspective. What other people are thinking and feeling must be imagined. That may not come naturally to certain individuals.

There is research on the function of brain cells called mirror neurons, which affect an individual's ability to empathize and understand what others are feeling (Oberman, Hubbard, McCleery, Altschuler, Pineda and Ramachandran, 2005). Mirror neurons work like this. If I saw an individual eating potato chips, that visual input would send a message to my mirror neurons, which would then send a message to my jaw muscles and cause me to act as if I were chewing potato chips along with the other person. The activation to my jaw muscle would be hard to detect with the naked eye, but nevertheless, I would actually be feeling what the other individual is feeling because I would essentially be imitating it in my brain. That is empathy: to feel what others feel.

Studies indicate that some individuals (especially those with autism spectrum disorders) have difficulty with the functioning of their mirror neurons (Oberman et al., 2005). The effect is that they will have difficulty taking other people's perspectives.

Most of us try to take others' perspectives all the time. That is what helps us to socialize in pleasing ways with them. We know when we have talked too long because we can feel the other's boredom. We know when we hurt others' feelings because we feel the hurt ourselves, prompting us to stop.

When perspective-taking does not come naturally, it makes it more likely to misinterpret others, which can lead to greater frustration and meltdowns.

I once had an eleven-year-old client who, besides having great difficulty understanding others' feelings, frequently misinterpreted his classmates' looks or comments, seeing them as threats. If other children looked at him because he raised his hand to answer a question in class, he thought they were staring at him and he would scream at them to stop looking. Similarly, if others said "hello" to him in the hallway, he perceived that they were making fun of him and he would yell or push them and then run under a chair and hide. His misinterpretations led to many meltdowns. With careful instruction on why kids looked at him or said hello, he was able to feel safer and not overreact.

Inflexibility

Many individuals can be remarkably inflexible in how they handle the daily challenges of life. This may be due in part to trouble with abstract thinking, as described above. When it is hard to use one's imagination, it becomes harder to solve new problems, and the likelihood of frustration increases which may lead to meltdowns. Certain learning disabilities, autism spectrum disorders, and types of cognitive impairment are associated with such inflexibility.

When it is hard to use one's imagination,
it becomes harder to solve new problems,
and the likelihood of frustration increases,
which may lead to meltdowns.

The issue of my own flexibility comes up every time I get driving directions from an online service. Although I get detailed, step-by-step directions of how to arrive at my destination, about 75% of the time I find that it tells me to turn onto a street that does not exist. If I had difficulty with my abstract thinking, I would be stuck at this point. It would be difficult to imagine what to do next if it was not on my printout of directions and my frustration would grow, perhaps to the point of a meltdown. With intact abstract thinking, I might think to ask for directions. For those who cannot brainstorm solutions to new problems, it is crucial to provide some preparation for anticipated challenging events. For example, if you give me driving directions, also give me your cell phone number and remind me to call if I get lost. This kind of preparation for the unknown is precisely the thrust of a good prevention plan; to provide someone with options to avoid what otherwise might have been a trigger to a meltdown.

An Explosive Combination

Imagine individuals who have a difficult temperament, are inflexible, and struggle to understand others' point of view. They come to new situations that are confusing, and do not have the problem-solving skills to handle them. Then they get overly upset, as if it were a life-threatening situation. This combination of emotional reactivity and lack of problem-solving ability is an equation for multiple meltdowns. These individuals are continually confronted with problematic events and cannot cope.

To address these difficulties, we must help children:

19

+ Find ways to calm themselves if a meltdown cannot be prevented (see Chapter 4: De-escalating a meltdown) and

+ Avoid other meltdowns by anticipating and preparing for triggering events.

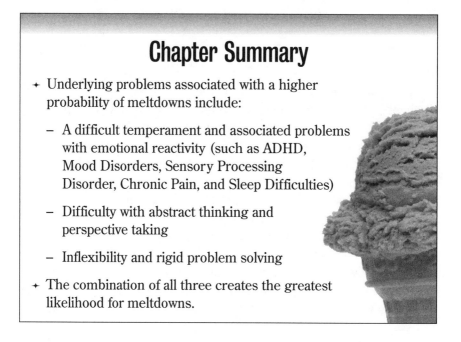

Chapter Summary

+ Underlying problems associated with a higher probability of meltdowns include:

 – A difficult temperament and associated problems with emotional reactivity (such as ADHD, Mood Disorders, Sensory Processing Disorder, Chronic Pain, and Sleep Difficulties)

 – Difficulty with abstract thinking and perspective taking

 – Inflexibility and rigid problem solving

+ The combination of all three creates the greatest likelihood for meltdowns.

THE SOLUTION

3

ACCEPTING AND APPRECIATING OUR CHILDREN

A wonderful essay written by Emily Perl Kingsley (1987) describes the experience of raising a child. She recounts having a baby as being like planning a special vacation to a beautiful location, such as Italy. You study Italian and plan all the great places to visit once in Italy. Finally, when the special day arrives and you get on the plane, you discover that the plane will actually land in Holland. You cannot believe, after all your plans, the airlines have diverted you. You heard everyone else talking of their past great trips to Italy and you feel tremendous disappointment. Yet you discover that Holland is not such a bad place—just not what you expected. And so now you busy yourself trying to discover all that Holland has to offer. If instead you spend all your time still wishing you were in Italy, you will never get to fully appreciate the joys of Holland.

This essay speaks to the importance of adjusting our expectations as parents so that we can truly appreciate and accept our children. It is only in the context of acceptance that we can help our children stretch themselves and learn new skills.

A parallel is found in the field of psychotherapy. In a recent review of 25 years of research into the outcome of psychotherapy, Lebow (2007) concludes that regardless of the type of therapeutic strategies used, most psychotherapy can be effective only when there is a strong, positive relationship between client and therapist. Some of the crucial factors that contribute to a positive relationship are acceptance, warmth, caring and the generation of hope or positive expectations.

How do we adjust our expectations so that we can develop and maintain a positive relationship with our own children? Three key issues are described below. We must:

+ Be able to control our own frustration before we can reduce our children's frustration.

+ Help our children feel competent with us and avoid "learned helplessness."

+ Avoid constant power struggles.

Controlling Our Own Frustration

First we must be able to do for ourselves what we need to do for our children. We need to control our own reactions to our children's challenging behaviors. Constantly expressing anger towards our children for behavior that they do not yet have the tools to manage only breaks down the relationship. The difference between being a bit irritated versus completely enraged by our children's behavior has to do with how well we do three things:

- Expect challenging behaviors from our children as part of normal development. When we expect perfect behavior, we set ourselves up to be enraged, rather than mildly annoyed, by our children's behavior.

- Do not see our children's actions as threats to our own competence, but instead recognize it as a function of their inability to cope with frustration. Alternatively, if we take it personally, our upset with ourselves increases our anger towards our children.

- Understand that challenging behaviors are temporary until we can figure out better ways to manage and prevent those difficult situations. If we see it as an unending problem, we will surely be angrier.

All the methods we use to help our children reduce their frustration are also methods we must use with ourselves, or else we will end up contributing to further escalation of frustration. We must learn to prevent our outbursts and find ways to calm ourselves when we lose our temper. By expecting and planning for frustrating situations with our children, we can avoid overreacting. When we know our own triggers, we can ready ourselves to respond in thoughtful ways rather than automatically losing our temper. As you read through this book for ways to help your children, consider how you can apply each strategy to yourself to be a more patient and confident parent or educator.

Building Competence

When children feel competent, they work harder and are more motivated to listen to us. In general, we build this sense of competence by offering ample praise and guiding them to activities that are within their range of abilities. Specifically, we can:

- Involve them in daily household activities such as gathering the laundry, setting the table, preparing dinner, or helping to clean up. Even if their participation makes the chore take longer, ask for their assistance and offer praise for their great help.

- Determine areas in which they have some natural strengths and set up activities in these areas (consider athletics, music, dance, art, or certain academic pursuits).

25

+ Avoid demands that are beyond their capabilities. Both at home and in school, we may need to modify the work demands so that we do not put students in the position of having to complete activities for which they are not ready. For example, students who are not yet reading or writing in early grades may need extra support, and should not be placed in embarrassing positions where they must perform beyond their ability in front of other students.

+ Praise their effort (rather than just their ability) when they are working on a project or attempting a new activity. We want them to appreciate the idea of working hard and practicing, more than whether or not they have succeeded. The lesson is: success eventually comes to those who work hard.

Avoiding Learned Helplessness

If, instead of planning for success, we put them in situations in which they cannot meet our expectations and we constantly criticize them, they become less motivated, less likely to listen, and develop "learned helplessness."

The concept of learned helplessness was first proposed by Martin Seligman in the 1960s as a model for human depression. Seligman and colleagues showed, first in animals and then with people, that when individuals repeatedly experience frustrating events that they cannot control, they eventually develop a sense of "learned helplessness" and tend to give up even when later confronted with events that they really can control. For example, in a classic experiment, students given unsolvable word puzzles, compared to those given solvable word puzzles, showed less motivation, more upset, and a greater likelihood of quitting when later confronted with challenging but solvable puzzles. In fact, their performance was similar to that of groups of students who were depressed. This early experience of failure can induce a sense of helplessness. Similarly, parents who continually criticize their children can instill a sense of helplessness in them—they feel that nothing they do is "right," so they stop trying. Examples of overly critical statements include:

+ "This is easy; why can't you do it? What's wrong with you?"

+ "All the other kids can do this."

+ "Just try harder," when children are failing at a task beyond their current ability. What they may really need is help in understanding what to do, or a more basic task to prepare them for the harder task.

Just being exposed to frustrating events such as criticism may not be enough to induce a helpless attitude. Many researchers have demonstrated that how one explains failure is crucial. If a person sees failure as a result of his lack of ability, this leads to a more helpless/depressed orientation, but if he explains failure as a result of lack of effort, it may result in greater motivation (Abramson et al., 1978). In fact, the students in the word puzzle experiment above exhibited a less depressed mood when they explained their trouble with the puzzles as due to lack of effort rather than to intellectual shortcomings.

Carol Dweck and her colleagues (Dweck, 1975; Diener & Dweck, 1978 & 1980) in a series of experiments have shown how some elementary students respond to frustrating work as a challenge and seem to enjoy it in an effort to learn more. In contrast, other children view frustration as a sign of personal inadequacy, and thus avoid challenging work, and develop a helpless attitude towards future work.

The 80/20 Rule

To help our children feel motivated and competent with us, we must first give them work they can achieve rather than unsolvable work. In the field of education, this is often referred to as the 80/20 rule. First give them the 80% work they can achieve before giving them the 20% that is more difficult for them. A concrete example of this comes from a study on the effects of how one orders test items on an exam. Firmen et al. (2004) showed that, when you put difficult test items before easier test items, students score lower and give up earlier than if you put the easier test items first. We must first build students' sense of "can do" before challenging them to help them stay motivated.

I recall when my own son began 1st grade and he was having difficulty learning to read. I tried too hard to teach him the sounds of all the letters and to begin sounding out words in the first month of 1st grade. In essence, I applied the exact opposite of the 80/20 rule, giving him very challenging work to do rather than beginning with work he could accomplish. I ended up turning him off to books and reading so that the mere sight of me began to anger him. I became associated with frustration and helplessness for him. Any efforts to read with him quickly escalated to meltdowns. When I finally got him help from gifted reading tutors, they applied the 80/20 rule, exposing him to tasks he could do in a game format. He regained his motivation to approach the skills of reading and began to progress. I backed off and, fortunately, he and I can now enjoy reading together.

Anticipating Frustration as Part of Learning

Elliott and Dweck (1988) have shown that they can induce children to become more focused on evaluating their "abilities" or, instead, focus on their "efforts" to learn, and this subsequently affects how they respond to challenging tasks. Those concentrating on their ability get frustrated more easily. In contrast, those attending to their level of effort respond to frustration with more motivation and positive feelings. Their research shows us that getting kids to think of ability as something that gradually changes with effort is key to reducing frustration and helplessness. In contrast, when kids see ability as a fixed entity that does not change, then frustrating tasks are seen as a sign of personal inadequacy.

As parents and teachers, we must help our youngsters to expect failure and frustration as an initial part of the learning process. Then we must instill a sense of hope that continued effort will help them get past these challenges. We must praise their continued efforts rather than simply praise their current ability.

Despite my pushing my son too fast with reading early on, I did at least understand that he would eventually learn with the right strategies. I impressed upon him from the beginning that reading is a skill that can be taught and "you are not supposed to be able to do it now, but with practice eventually you will." I told him about my uncle who was unable to read for the first several years of grade school and initially became very frustrated. But because he never gave up, with practice he learned to read and eventually became a talented college professor. I tried to give my son hope

28

and a vision of the long-term effort involved in learning to read. As a result, he persisted in his efforts and learned to read proficiently.

When to Avoid Power Struggles

Constant power struggles create stress for everyone and slowly break down the relationship between adult and child. One of the toughest questions parents and teachers ask is when should they push a child to do something and when should they avoid a power struggle. My rule of thumb is:

If children are prepared for a challenge and have been taught skills to cope with that situation, then we can try to push through their resistance and endure the power struggle. If children do not have the skills to cope with a challenging task, then we should avoid the power struggle.

For example, if a child resists homework, but we have simplified the tasks involved, taught him or her to ask for help or for a break if necessary, and we are starting at a reasonable hour, then we can feel more comfortable withholding playtime until the child cooperates in doing schoolwork. On the other hand, if a student is resistant and the work is at a level that is too difficult, and he has not been taught how to ask for help, then it would not be wise to engage in the power struggle.

The following story demonstrates the futility of engaging in an escalating power struggle with a child who is not prepared for a challenging situation. In an inner-city school system where I worked years ago, there was a 5th grader with reading problems. On weekends, he attended a recreation program run by a man who taught me more about developing positive relationships than any book I read or graduate school training I had. He became a big daddy to a lot of fatherless children and knew how to help them feel valued and competent. His recreation program offered supervision for sports, arts and crafts and academic work, but made no demands on the students to perform in any of these areas. In general, the program offered a place to relax and feel supported, praised, but not pushed to perform for a grade, as was the case during the school week.

During the week, this man worked as the security guard at the school. The particular fifth grade boy in question had modifications to his language arts class from a teacher who understood his difficulties with reading. One day, as she often did, she told the class, "Take out your language arts folder and do the following three paragraphs," and then whispered to the boy to just do one of the paragraphs, which he accepted because he knew she was choosing the work that he could do. However, the next day there was a substitute teacher who said, "Take out your language arts folder and do the following three paragraphs; your teacher told me you did not finish this yesterday." His hand went up and he said, "I don't have to do this." She said, "You have to do it just like everyone else." He became angry and shouted, "No I don't, and you can't make me do it!" As the student began to feel threatened, she too began to feel threatened, and worried that she would have a mutiny on her hands if she did not take a stand, so she became angry and said sternly, "You need to do the work like everyone else, young man!" He got more angry and shouted again "You can't force me to do anything!" She then did what many substitutes do in that situation; she sent him to the principal.

Now the principal had already seen nine kids that day. With all nine kids he told them that they needed to do their work or else they would miss recess and their parents would be informed. All nine out of nine kids did what they were told. They just needed an authority, who they knew would follow through, to reiterate the rules and discipline plan. However, this boy was different.

When he came down to the principal's office, already agitated, the principal said, gently as he did to all the others, that he must do his work or miss recess and have his parents called. He yelled, "I don't have to do that work and you can't make me!" Now, truthfully, he did not have to do the work, according to the modification plan that was in force, allowing him changes to his language arts curriculum—but with the regular teacher out, no one knew this.

The principal couldn't believe the boy's harsh tone of voice and was thinking that this boy would be going to middle school next year and needed to learn here and now how to respect authority. The principal asserted, "Young man, you may not talk to me this way. When you are in this building you must respect all the adults. It is as if we are your parents during the school day." The boy reacted, "YOU ARE NOT MY FATHER!" standing a bit too close now to the principal. If things had continued like this, the boy might have shown the principal his middle finger (as he had once in the past) prompting the principal to suspend him, which would only serve to teach the boy a reliable way to get out of school.

Instead, the security guard saw the escalating power struggle as he passed by the office and intervened. The principal knew the security guard had a way with children and did not mind letting him take over. The security guard said to the boy "You're right; you really should not have to do that work." The boy's temper calmed a bit as he perked up and listened to the security guard. The two of them walked and talked about TV shows and other interests until the boy was calm, and then the guard (also unaware of the modifications the boy was entitled to) convinced the boy to do some of the language arts he did not even have to do. The guard was able to do this because he knew how to handle the situation, to deal with the emotion before using any reasoning.

What this guard initially did to avert a meltdown was to validate the boy's feelings rather than continue in the power struggle. A very popular book, titled *How to Talk to Kids so Kids Will Listen*, describes essentially this process of showing understanding and empathy for children's feelings before they will listen (Faber and Mazlish, 1999). Words one can use include:

+ "That makes sense."
+ "I can understand how you feel."
+ "I wish I could make it better."

To avoid an escalating power struggle, we may need to deal with the emotions before we can use reason and enforce rules. Sometimes we do this by making validating comments to our children and sometimes we find ways to distract them from the triggers to their upset.

More ways to calm children in the throes of a meltdown are addressed in the next chapter.

Chapter Summary

+ When we accept and appreciate our children, we help to establish a positive relationship through which we can help them to learn. The following strategies all involve ways in which we may have to adjust our expectations of our children so we can maintain a good relationship.

+ Control our own frustration by:

- Expecting challenging behaviors from our children as part of normal development.

- Realizing our children's challenging behaviors are not threats to our own competence, but instead are a function of the youngsters' tenuous ability to cope with frustration.

- Understanding that challenging behaviors are temporary until we can find better ways to manage and prevent those difficult situations.

+ Plan for children to approach simpler, confidence-building tasks before challenging them with more difficult tasks.

+ Teach them to expect frustration as part of learning rather than a sign of failure.

+ Avoid power struggles when the child does not yet have the skills to cope with a particular situation.

4

DE-ESCALATING
A MELTDOWN

A seventh-grade boy was in the car with his mother driving to my office one afternoon. They passed by a video store and the boy said to his mother, "Mom, I have to stop, there's a new video game that came out." Mom said, "No, we're late for Dr. Baker's appointment." The boy said, "But you don't understand, it just came out and I need to get it now." She said, "You didn't tell me before and now we're late." Then, as they passed the video store, he said, "OOOH, I hate you. Turn back now!" She ignored him at this point, while he continued to fume.

Upon arriving at my office, he began to pace and said, "This sucks, I hate being here, I hate this office." His mother explained that he hadn't gotten to go to the video store. I asked Mom if we could promise to take him right after the session. She agreed and I told him, "Great news! Mom said if you work with me now, she is going to take you to the video store right after the session." He seemed not to hear and continued to pace and grumble about how he hated this place and that everything stinks. Mom was exasperated after the car ride and the continued meltdown in my office. She gave up on promises and instead began to threaten him. "If you don't calm down now, I will never in your lifetime take you to the video store!" she said. He did not seem to even hear her. He was in the meltdown zone and Mom was not far behind him.

I recalled that he enjoyed playing the card game Uno, and I commented, "I'm going to play Uno." He replied, "I'm not playing!" I said, "That's okay, I am going to play with Mom."

Mom was good at looking as though she didn't know how to play. She remarked, "I'm not sure what card to play; I might lose." The boy peeked over at her cards, and without a word he picked up the cards for her. Now I was playing with him. Although he was a terrible sport and needed help in dealing with losing, I decided against working on that at the moment. On this day, I let him win. Suddenly he smiled and was in a good mood. He was back from meltdown mode.

Now that the crisis was averted, Mom understandably wanted to make sure this problem would not happen again. She tried to make a plan for next time so he would not melt down every time someone said no. She said to him, "Now that you're calm, lets talk about this video store thing." His face changed and, within moments, he was pacing and yelling, "This sucks, I hate being here ..." You cannot go back and discuss past problems with some individuals, especially when their negative feelings are still fresh. How could we make a plan and help prevent future problems like this if we could not talk about it with the child?

I helped him prepare for future moments in which he would not get what he wanted without ever mentioning the blowup about the video store. After more Uno and other distractions, I began to make a plan with him for next time with no mention of what had happened earlier. I told him, "next week when you come to the office you might pass McDonalds"—I did not dare say anything about the video store—"and you might want to go there, but your Mom may say no because she wants to have dinner somewhere else. If you are cool with that and don't get angry, she may be so happy that she lets you have dessert at home and play your computer games." Now the truth is, he always got his computer games; we were just highlighting for him that he would get this when he accepted no for an answer about McDonalds. To accept no and not see it as the end of the world, children must be able to focus on the positive events that are still to come so they have some reason to continue to control themselves.

How to De-escalate a Meltdown

1. Use distraction to avert the escalation of angry, out-of-control emotions when reasoning, logic, threats, and punishments have not worked.

2. These are *temporary crisis tools* to employ when our children are out of control; they are not substitutes for eventually doing the harder work of understanding why the meltdown occurred and creating a prevention plan as described in Chapters 5-10.

3. When the same meltdowns repeat themselves, develop a plan so the problem does not happen again. When discussing a plan, you may decide not to rehash the negative behaviors that already occurred. Some children can handle this; some cannot. You need to know your child.

Distractions

There are many ways to distract from and de-escalate a meltdown. For children below the age of four, it may not take too much to distract them away from that which is upsetting them. Showing them an interesting toy, handing them a favorite stuffed animal or book, looking out the window, turning on the TV, or just a hug and a bounce on a parent's lap can serve as quick distractions.

As children age, all those distractions can continue to work, but may not engage their attention enough to keep them from the situation that is upsetting them. Instead, consider those things that most engage your child's attention. For the student in the above example, it was the card game Uno I knew he loved. If you know a child's passion, it can be the most effective distraction.

Once two older middle school students were about to fight each other in a group I was facilitating. One was crying because he had been teased by someone outside the group. Another boy in the group called him a baby for crying. They began to argue, and would not respond to my efforts to get their attention and resolve the argument. I got in between them, but they moved to get back in each other's faces. Just as they were going to square off for what I believed would have been a fist fight, I pulled out a pack of Yu-Gi-Oh cards that I always keep handy in case of such emergencies. Both students were collectors and players of the game cards. As soon as I took them out and said, "Hey guys, do either of you have any of these cards?" they stopped arguing, looked up and focused on the cards. As we discussed the relative value of each card, I suggested quietly that they apologize to each other and that we could talk about teasing on another day. They mumbled their quick apologies and refocused on the cards. I avoided the subject of teasing for the rest of the group and did not take it up again until the next group session when it was not as raw for either of them.

Here are some suggestions for distracting and calming your children.

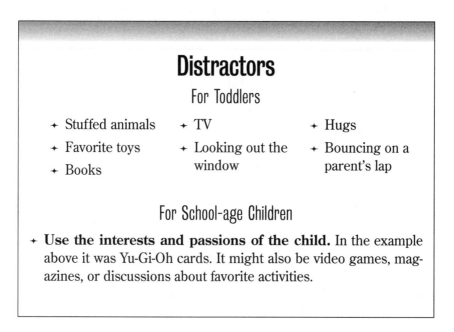

Distractors

For Toddlers

- Stuffed animals
- Favorite toys
- Books
- TV
- Looking out the window
- Hugs
- Bouncing on a parent's lap

For School-age Children

- **Use the interests and passions of the child.** In the example above it was Yu-Gi-Oh cards. It might also be video games, magazines, or discussions about favorite activities.

+ **Use humor** to get the child to smile or laugh and distract from what is upsetting. One has to be careful that the child does not think you are making fun of him or her. To ensure this, I often ask, "Is it okay if I try to make you laugh to get your mind off of this?" If the child refuses, I will not pursue this tactic.

+ **Validate their feelings** so they feel understood (see Farber & Mazlish, 1999). For example:

"I found math hard too. I wish you didn't have to do this."

"Yeah, I hate when you have to wait for what you want."

"I understand how much you wanted to win. It was really important to you."

"I can see why you got so mad that you wanted to push her, especially since she bugged you first … but it's not okay for either of you to push each other."

Myles and Southwick (2005) offer many similar strategies to avert or de-escalate meltdown moments. Here are some of their suggestions I have found useful:

+ **Have the child be a messenger**. This can be useful in a classroom setting. When a student is starting to get agitated, send him or her to give an important message to the school nurse to distract from the upsetting events.

+ **Get closer to the child**. Sometimes getting closer to the child and/or touching the child in order to let the child know you are there can help. This can be useful when the meltdown is not triggered by the adult's behavior, as when a child is frustrated with work or a game.

+ **Use a secret signal**. A teacher or parent could have a secret signal such as a look or a cough to tell the child that he is beginning to get agitated and should watch their behavior.

+ **Create a written schedule of routines.** This involves furnishing the child with visual reminders of her schedule to provide comfort in understanding what to expect next. It may help her focus away from her upset, and on comforting routines yet to come.

+ **Create a home base.** This involves making a safe, comforting place for children to go when they are feeling upset. For example, one can create a beanbag area with favorite books and stuffed animals in a bedroom or in a classroom. If children overuse such a location in order to avoid doing work, then strive to create a prevention plan that will make the work more agreeable (see Chapter 7).

+ **Just walk and don't talk** refers to walking with the child away from the situation that upset them, allowing him to vent without confronting him or saying anything that could further inflame the meltdown.

When Too Much Distraction Can Make Things Worse

When a problem behavior repeats itself over and over again, it always makes sense to try to understand why it occurs and develop a prevention plan to avoid these repeat problems (see Chapter 6). Distraction should not be the preferred strategy for repeat problems; it should be reserved for emergency situations in which the meltdown cannot be prevented, no plan is in place, and the behavior is escalating rapidly.

There are times when overusing distractions can actually worsen the situation. Let's say a child is yelling and falling to the floor in an effort to avoid challenging work and we then allow him or her to play a favorite game to calm down. This will likely reward the tantrum and make it more likely that the child will engage in those behaviors again to avoid work. Thus when distraction is used when children are avoiding work, it may perpetuate the problem. The real work is not in calming the meltdown of the moment, but in learning why they are avoiding the work, developing a plan to make it more agreeable, and giving them other ways to cope with the challenging work, such as asking for help.

Sometimes it is hard to know in the moment of a meltdown whether the child is really trying to avoid work or something else is going on. Thus I am not opposed to using distraction *one time* in a situation that leads to work avoidance, as long as we make a plan to prevent the future occurrence of those meltdowns.

The one-time rule for avoidance

1. Distraction is a crisis tool. It can be used for calming a meltdown when we do not have a plan already in place.

2. If distraction allows a child to avoid a task, we should *use it only once* with that particular task. Overuse will make it more likely for the child to melt down again to avoid the task. Instead, we must develop a prevention plan to make the task more tolerable, and teach the child better ways to handle frustration—such as learning to ask for help or for a break (see Chapter 7).

Helping Children Find Their Own Calming Strategies

Just as we may use distraction techniques to interrupt a meltdown, we want to teach our children to do this for themselves. They will not always be in a position where they can rely on someone else to calm them and, thus, they will need to develop strategies of their own.

Ultimately, the most effective long-term approach to helping children keep calm involves creating prevention plans to deal with specific triggers to their meltdowns as described in Chapters 6-10. This way they can avoid getting angry to begin with. Because one cannot always know ahead of time what will trigger a meltdown, it is helpful to have a general calming strategy that a child can use in any situation.

There is plenty of evidence that children can learn general calming strategies to help them think before they act. Some of this research comes from studies looking at the effects of social-emotional learning programs (SEL) in schools, where children are taught about their emotions, how to calm themselves, as well as learning ways to solve interpersonal problems. Daniel Goleman's book on emotional intelligence (1995) summarizes much of this research, which points to gains in self-control by children who participate in these programs.

The first step of many of these SEL programs is to help children develop ways to stop and calm down before deciding how to solve a problem. I have found that the best calming strategies come from talking with children to find out what works best for them. Do they like taking deep breaths or do they find that drawing or reading is more calming? This discussion should take place during calm moments, not during a meltdown. Learning cannot occur during meltdown moments. Calming strategies must be practiced before they get upset if there is to be any possibility of using calming techniques once they are upset. To help them begin to calm themselves, I recommend the following steps:

Steps for Creating Self-Calming Strategies

1. When they are focused and calm, talk with them about how they know when they are getting upset. Help them identify internal cues for these feelings. Write them down or draw them. If they are going to self-calm, they will need to know when they are getting angry before they reach a full-blown meltdown.

2. Talk with them about things that soothe and calm them. Make an agreement to practice these calming strategies so they can use them when they are upset. The list might include:

+ Taking deep breaths
+ Counting to 10
+ Taking a walk

+ Getting a drink of water, or sucking on ice cubes
+ Chewing on a straw or gum

+ Drawing
+ Listening to music
+ Reading
+ Watching TV
+ Athletic activities

+ Holding a favorite toy, squeeze ball, or stuffed animal
+ Rocking in a rocking chair
+ Swinging on a swingset

3. Create a plan for home and school indicating which calming strategies they will use.

4. Decide whom they will talk with to discuss how to solve the problem once they are calm.

5. Each day for several months, have the child imagine the sensations of anger and rehearse the calming strategy. He will have to be able to do the calming strategy without too much conscious effort, because he may have difficulty thinking as he is beginning to get angry. Parents can rehearse their home strategy each morning or after school. Teachers can have their students rehearse their calming plan every morning five minutes before class begins.

The form on the following page can be used to help you create a general calming plan for your child.

General Calming Plan Form

Feeling Upset

How do I know when I am upset? _____
_____
_____
_____
_____

Home Plan

What calms me down at home? _____
_____
_____
_____
_____

Whom can I talk to at home to help solve the problem? _____
_____
_____
_____
_____

School Plan

What calms me down at school? _____
_____
_____
_____
_____

Whom can I talk to at school to help solve the problem?_____
_____
_____
_____

This chapter has only focused on ways to calm a meltdown in the moment. To help prevent the meltdowns in the first place, we will need to develop prevention plans that are specific to certain triggers. That is the issue we turn to next.

Chapter Summary

+ Distraction is a key tool in helping individuals calm down.

+ Types of distractions and related calming strategies include:

– Using the interests and hobbies of the child.
– Using humor
– Validating feelings so the child feels understood
– Playing with stuffed animals or favorite toys
– Looking out the window
– Bouncing on a parent's lap
– Using books, TV, videos
– Getting hugs

+ Myles and Southwick (2005) offer similar strategies to avert or de-escalate meltdown moments:

– Have the child be a messenger.
– Get closer to the child. Use a secret signal.
– Use a written schedule of routines
– Create a home base
– Just walk and don't talk

+ If distraction allows a child to avoid a task, we should use it only once with that particular task. Overuse will make it more likely that the child will melt down again to avoid the task. We must develop a prevention plan to make the task more tolerable and teach the child better ways to handle frustration.

+ Children can learn ways to calm themselves before or after they melt down. These are general calming strategies that can be used in many situations. Yet the most effective strategies will be the prevention plans created to deal with specific triggering situations (as described in Chapters 6-10).

5

UNDERSTANDING WHY REPEAT PROBLEMS OCCUR

To get to a point where we are no longer just calming the waters in the midst of a storm, we need to understand how to predict and prevent the storm itself. We now turn our attention to exploring the triggers of a repeat meltdown.

Every day at recess a third grader named Kevin has challenges controlling himself. He hits, pushes, kicks, and argues with the other students, remaining angry for hours afterwards. When confronted about his behavior, he gets even angrier, crying and yelling at adults or running away from them.

His teacher tries to help by offering him a prize each day from a classroom treasure chest if he keeps his hands to himself at recess. He expresses great interest in earning these prizes but nevertheless, each day he returns from recess frustrated that once again he has had some physical altercation and did not earn the prize. When the principal explains that he will be punished for his behavior and lose recess the next day, his upset escalates and he stays angry for hours, yelling and screaming or trying to run away. His parents have offered him rewards when he controls himself and have removed privileges when he loses control at recess. Despite consistent rules, rewards, and consequences, the problems continue. Here, traditional discipline has not been enough. We need to understand why Kevin keeps having these problems at recess.

Understanding the Triggers

The process for understanding why repeat problem behaviors occur has a fancy name in the behavioral literature. It's called "Functional Behavioral Assessment." Don't let the technical name intimidate you; it means no more than trying to understand what causes and perpetuates a problem. The word *function* refers to the idea that the problem behavior serves some function, such as allowing the child to avoid a tough situation, get attention from others, or vent frustration, for example. When creating a prevention plan, what the behavior looks like (whether the child hits or yells) will be less important than the function the behavior serves. For example, if a child hits in order to try to get others to play with him, a prevention plan will involve teaching the child better ways to ask others to play. If, on the other hand, the child hits to get people to leave him alone, then a prevention plan will involve teaching him different ways to ask people not to bother him. The same behavior, hitting, can lead us to different ways to help a child based on the "function" of the behavior.

ABCs of Behavior: Antecedent, Behavior, Consequence

To assess why a problem behavior occurs, we need to know about the circumstances surrounding the behavior. This is often referred to as the ABCs of the behavior. "A" stands for antecedents or what happens before the behavior. "B" stands for the behavior itself, what the child did or said that was problematic. And "C" stands for consequences, which does not necessarily mean punishment, but rather what happened after the behavior occurred. Essentially, "antecedent, behavior, and consequence" refers to "before, during, and after." Getting information about what happened before the behavior gives us clues as to what may have triggered the problem. Information about what happened after the behavior sheds light on whether there is something rewarding about the behavior (i.e., a hidden payoff).

For example, let's look again at Kevin's behavior during recess. We might discover that one of his triggers (an antecedent) is when kids argue with him about a call during a game at recess (such as whether he is "out" or "safe" in kickball). Kevin might get mad and push others when arguing a call. If, as a consequence of pushing other children, the other kids gave in to Kevin, we might say that there is a rewarding pay-off for his aggressive behavior. But if the children did not give in to him and, in fact, stop playing with him, it would appear that his aggression is not being rewarded. In the next section we shall investigate what really did cause Kevin's aggressive behavior at recess.

Getting the ABCs: Interviews and Observations

In an effort to find out the ABCs of the problem behavior, we can often start with an interview of those who saw the behavior. If we cannot get enough information from an interview, we often need to observe the behavior ourselves. The following table outlines some of what to look for in investigating what the antecedents, behavior and consequences are for a particular problem behavior. The ABC Diary that follows shows how to create a written record of our observations so that we can later look for patterns that reveal what may be causing the problem behaviors.

What to Ask or Observe
When Seaching for the ABCs

Antecedent: What triggered the behavior? Consider:

+ **Sensory stimulation.** These include the level of noise, light, touch, smell, taste, movement, or other forms of stimulation that might be upsetting to the individual.

+ **Lack of structure.** Were instructions clear about what to do? Were there visual reminders of what to do, or only verbal instructions? Without enough structure, children can become confused.

+ **Internal or biological triggers.** These might include hunger, pain, illness, or tiredness that might contribute to a meltdown.

+ **Demands.** These include directions to do work, or social expectations to converse, play or interact with others.

+ **Waiting.** This involves situations in which children do not get what they want immediately, or cannot get what they want at all, or have to stop doing something they like.

+ **Threats to self-image.** This involves situations that cause children to feel ashamed or embarrassed, such as losing a game, making mistakes, being criticized, or getting teased.

+ **Unmet wishes for attention.** These include moments when others refuse to play or interact with them, when they are jealous of others, or when they fear being alone.

Behavior: What did the child do or say in the situation?

+ **Describe the behavior using detailed, concrete terms** rather than abstract words. A good detailed description would be: "My son pushed another child's shoulder and said, 'I hate you.'" In contrast, an unclear description would be "My son got angry and physical with another child." In this last sentence, we really do not know what was said or how he was physical with the other child.

Consequence: What happened after the behavior occurred?

Describe in detail what others did and said after the child's behavior occurred. Consider whether the child's behavior resulted in:

+ **Avoiding a situation**. Sometimes children stall, make excuses, or tantrum to avoid difficult work, a social demand, or seemingly fun situations that might be overly stimulating (e.g., refusing to go to a party at an amusement park).

+ **Getting others' attention**. Sometimes children demonstrate challenging behaviors to get others to play, laugh, or help them with something. Children might start wrestling with their parents, running away from them, or tell made-up stories. If the child initially looks happy and is smiling, this may be a clue that the behavior is an attempt to play rather than to avoid a frustrating task.

+ **Getting some desired object**. Children may ask repeatedly for food, toys, or a privilege, and then tantrum if they do not get what they want immediately.

+ **Self-pleasure or soothing**. These are often repetitive behaviors that do not seem to have an impact on others but serve to entertain, provide pleasure, or soothe the child. Examples include self-talk, fidgeting, tapping, rocking, and even masturbation. Although the behavior may be upsetting to others, the child is using the behavior to soothe or entertain himself.

+ **Venting of frustration**. Sometimes a child's behavior has no clear benefit, in that it does not lead to avoiding an unpleasant task, or garner desired attention. Instead, the behavior seems to be a way of venting frustration. One example is when a child gets frustrated with a project, begins to destroy the project, yet refuses to quit trying or accept help.

Blank ABC Diary (to keep track of the ABCs)

Date/Time	Antecedents/Triggers	Behavior	Consequences

Returning to Kevin's problems at recess, I began to explore the ABCs of his problem behaviors. We already knew what the Cs were: he consistently lost recess and home privileges for physical altercations at recess, or alternatively received rewards and home privileges if he behaved well at recess. To get more information about the specific behavior and the antecedents, I started by interviewing his teacher. I asked first about what he did. She said he has kicked, hit, and pushed other children at recess. I asked her to tell me about the most recent example. She said yesterday he reportedly pushed another boy in the shoulder during recess time.

Now that I had a clear explanation of what he did, I inquired about the triggers (antecedents) of this behavior. I asked, "What was happening just before he pushed the boy?" She said, "I don't know, I was not at recess with them; only the lunch aides are." So I decided to ask the lunch aides if they saw what Kevin did yesterday. They said, "Honestly, Dr. Baker, we have 75 children out here, and by the time we find out about something it usually has already happened. Do you really expect us to keep track of every situation?"

I was not getting very far with my interviews. I tried asking the other children. They said Kevin just walked up to another boy and pushed him. I asked, "What was the other boy doing before Kevin pushed him?" They said, "Nothing; he just pushed him." Again I was striking out with getting the triggering information. I asked Kevin himself if he remembered what was happening at recess, and he just denied that he pushed anyone despite everyone else saying he did.

My interview did not yield enough useful information for me to understand what was happening. I went on to the observation stage. I planned to observe him briefly at recess knowing I might well see something since these problems happened almost every day.

At recess I saw Kevin go up to two children playing checkers and ask, "Can I play?" They said, "No, we just started." He squinted his eyes, grunting angrily as he lightly shoved one of the children. I asked him why he did that. He said, "Because they hate me and won't let me play." That taught me a lot about what might be triggering him. He perceived that peers disliked him when they said he could not play. I had interpreted the response he got from the peers quite differently. I thought the boys meant that he could not play immediately because checkers is a two-person game and thus he must wait to play the winner.

I wanted to see whether my guess about Kevin's sensitivity to rejection was accurate. So I watched him a bit longer at recess on this day and the next day. I noticed that when peers said he could not play he was likely to get angry and hit, push or kick them, when much of the time it seemed to me the peers were really just indicating that he needed to wait and play the winner or wait until the next game started so they could choose new players.

I noticed one other consistent trigger that seemed to make him upset. When he disagreed about a questionable call during a game, the argument often escalated into a physical shoving match. In one instance, he was playing foursquare. He hit the ball and one of his peers said the ball went out of bounds. Kevin insisted the ball was in fair play. The two boys argued until Kevin pushed the other boy. At that point, a lunch aide saw what was happening and took him by the arm, escorting him to the principal's office. There he waited until the principal saw him and explained how needed to keep hands to himself, and made it clear that Kevin would miss recess the next day. Kevin tried to explain how the other boy lied when he said Kevin's ball was out of bounds, but the principal maintained that no matter what others do, Kevin was not allowed to touch other children.

Over the two short recess periods that I observed Kevin, all the incidences of physical aggression had the same kind of triggers. They always seemed to follow times in which others rejected his attempts to join in or argued about a call. Sometimes the altercations were noticed by lunch aides and he was punished; other times they went unnoticed. Never did it seem that his aggression convinced peers that he was right about a call or helped him to join in. If anything, peers were now wary of Kevin and seemed to steer clear of him.

Some of these events are shown in the sample ABC Diary I recorded of my observations of Kevin at recess on the first day (see below).

ABC Diary for Kevin

Date/Time	Antecedents/Triggers	Behavior	Consequences
11/3 11:40 a.m.	Kevin walks up to two boys and asks if he can play checkers with them. They say, "No we just started."	Kevin squints his eyes and pushes one of the boys and then walks away.	The other boy ignores him.
	I ask Kevin why he did this.	He says, "Because the boys hate me and will not let me play."	I try to explain that they may just want Kevin to wait until the game is done.
11/3 11:51 a.m.	Kevin is playing foursquare with other peers. His ball lands close to the line and one of the other boys says Kevin's ball was out of bounds.	Kevin argues that his ball was in bounds, raising his voice at the other boy.	The other boy yells back, "You're out, Kevin, sit down." The other kids do not say anything.

11/3 11:52 a.m.	Kevin and the other boy continue to argue, yelling at each other.	Kevin pushes the boy to the ground.	The other boy gets up and approaches Kevin. The other kids start to circle around them and the lunch aide sees this, asks the kids what happened, and they say Kevin pushed the other boy. The lunch aide escorts Kevin to the principal's office where he is told he will miss recess the next day.

Seeing the Pattern

In reviewing the ABCs of Kevin's behavior at recess, we began to see a pattern. Two types of situations seemed to be consistent triggers: (1) being rejected when attempting to join in, and (2) arguments about questionable calls. In the first instance Kevin seemed to interpret the rejection personally, feeling that others hate him, which made him angry and want to retaliate. He failed to see that peers did not actually dislike him; they just wanted him to wait to play in the next game. In the second instance, Kevin seemed frustrated when he believed there was an unjust call. He retaliated against this perceived injustice.

In neither of these situations did it appear that Kevin was getting some hidden payoff. Looking at the consequences of his actions, the aggressive behaviors resulted in punishment from both peers and adults, so we cannot say the behaviors allowed him to get his way. The focus of our prevention plan then could not just focus on altering disciplinary measures, as he already had a discipline plan to discourage him from being aggressive. Unfortunately, discipline alone was not working. Kevin's reaction to these situations made it difficult for him to think clearly about the consequences of his behavior. The prevention plan will need to focus on altering the triggers to his upset, and on how he perceives these triggers.

In the next chapter we will examine how to create a good prevention plan in general, and what we did to help Kevin, in particular.

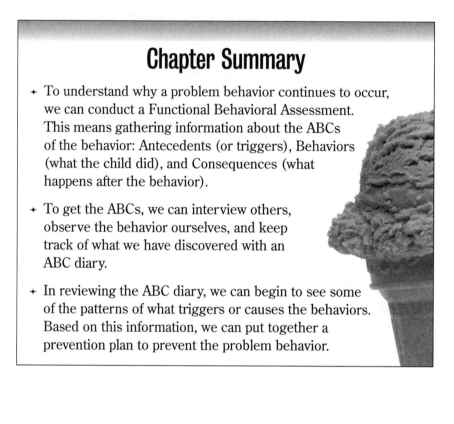

Chapter Summary

+ To understand why a problem behavior continues to occur, we can conduct a Functional Behavioral Assessment. This means gathering information about the ABCs of the behavior: Antecedents (or triggers), Behaviors (what the child did), and Consequences (what happens after the behavior).

+ To get the ABCs, we can interview others, observe the behavior ourselves, and keep track of what we have discovered with an ABC diary.

+ In reviewing the ABC diary, we can begin to see some of the patterns of what triggers or causes the behaviors. Based on this information, we can put together a prevention plan to prevent the problem behavior.

6

CREATING A PREVENTION PLAN

For minor, one-time issues with your children, there is no need to create a comprehensive prevention plan. For example, if your child always brushes their teeth at night and one night they refuse to do it, this does not call for a thorough assessment of why such a problem occurred. In contrast, when you have a repeated problem with your youngster, who has not responded to the usual dose of rules and consequences, it makes sense to try to understand why the problem persists and to create a good prevention plan. Such was the case with Kevin (described in the previous chapter).

In this chapter, I lay out a general model to guide you in creating prevention plans for any repeated problems you encounter with your children. I will show how this model was applied to Kevin's persistent recess problem. Then, in Chapters 7-10, we will apply this same model to some of the most common situations in which children experience meltdowns.

Components of a Good Prevention Plan

The following four components should be considered when creating an effective prevention plan:

CHANGE THE TRIGGERS

How can we change the triggering situations to make it less likely for the challenging behavior to occur? We might change the following aspects of the situation:

+ **Sensory stimulation.** Alter the noise, light, smell, taste or touch sensation in the situation. Some children may need quieter environments to work in. Certain individuals find fluorescent lighting to be distracting, and function better with incandescent lighting. Some children find certain textures of foods and specific odors offensive or cannot tolerate the feel of certain types of clothing. In contrast, other children may crave certain types of sensation, getting bored easily unless there are high levels of stimulation. See Kranowitz (2006) for a full description of sensory modifications.

+ **Timing of the situation.** Change when we ask a child to do something so that they are not excessively hungry, tired, or sick when confronting a challenging task.

+ **Task difficulty.** Make a challenging task easier or shorter in duration.

+ **Visual supports.** Use pictures or written words to increase understanding of learning material or remind students of the steps involved in completing a task. Examples include posters or cue cards that depict rules, or graphic organizers that display information in a web format to increase comprehension and later recall of stories or factual information.

TEACH SKILLS TO DEAL WITH THE TRIGGERS

What alternative skills can we teach the child to better cope with the situations that trigger problem behaviors or meltdowns? The short list below shows some skills to teach for different kinds of triggers and problem behaviors.

Triggering Situation	Problem Behavior	Alternative Skills*
Demands: Difficult work, chores, sensory challenges, new situations and/or social demands	Avoidance or refusal to participate.	Learning to ask for help, to watch others do the task, to negotiate how much to do or how to alter a challenging task. (See Chapter 7)
Waiting: Being denied some activity or object or having to wait a long time for it.	Demands, tantrums, or retaliation.	Learning the "invisible payoff" of waiting or accepting no: others will be happy and give you something you want later if you can wait (see Chapter 8).
Threats to self-image: Teasing, criticism, losing a game and making mistakes	Taking it personally as a negative judgment about oneself and one's abilities.	Learning not to perceive these events as judgments about one's own ability or character, but instead see it as a reflection of the other person's issues or a chance to learn more. (See Chapter 9).
Unmet wishes for attention: Wanting to play or interact with others. Fear of being alone.	Annoying others to get them to interact. Complaining that others get more attention. Clinging to others.	Learning effective ways to initiate play, understanding that one is valued even when they are not getting attention, and learning to self-soothe rather than depend on others (see Chapter 10).

* Many of these lessons are summarized in Chapters 7-10. A more comprehensive set of skill lessons appear in my social skills books (Baker, 2003; 2005).

TRY REWARD OR LOSS SYSTEMS

This refers to rewarding the positive, alternative skills and, under certain circumstances, using a loss of privilege for engaging in disruptive behaviors.

+ **Rewards** might include praise; material rewards such as access to a toy, special food, or favored games; or point systems that add up to larger rewards like buying a new toy or going on a special outing.

+ **Losses** might involve ignoring the behavior or taking away a privilege, such as TV, computer time, or being grounded. Loss systems should be used only if the triggering situation has been modified, the child has been taught a better way to deal with the situation and was reminded to engage in the positive behavior, but instead chose the disruptive behavior.

CONSIDER BIOLOGICAL AND PHYSICAL STRATEGIES

+ **Dietary changes** to reduce irritability and increase self-control. Certain allergies can cause chronic pain and irritation that may increase irritability. Reducing these allergens may decrease frustration level overall. Many unproven "cure-all" diets exist, so it pays to have specific allergy tests done to make sure that the dietary adjustments are necessary. There is also some research suggesting that certain supplements (omega-3 fatty acids from fish oil) may increase attention and improve learning among children with attention problems (Sinn & Bryan, 2007).

+ **Exercise, meditation and other physical modes of relaxation.** There is a wealth of data on the mood-enhancing effects of vigorous exercise and the long-term benefit to learning and memory. Similar studies are beginning to emerge on the impact of meditation practices. Enhanced mood and greater attention and learning all suggest exercise can reduce frustration. A recent article in *Newsweek* magazine summarizes much of the research on the effects of exercise on the brain (Carmichael, March, 2007).

✦ **Medications that can alter impulse control and mood.** Medication can be an important tool in improving behavior, but given side effects and the lack of studies on the long-term effects in children, it should not be the first thing we pursue. All of the interventions described above should be utilized before we seek an evaluation for medication. If changing the triggers and teaching skills fail to work, and the behavior is of crisis proportion (e.g., the child is at risk of being thrown out of school or is making repeated suicidal threats) then seeking an evaluation for medication can be a valid consideration. A qualified doctor should carefully assess the symptoms and then monitor both beneficial and negative side effects of medication throughout treatment. This means that doctors should be getting direct feedback about the effects of the medicine from parental reports, school reports, and any lab tests, to evaluate levels of the medicine or potential side effects.

A Prevention Plan for Kevin

In Kevin's case, we focused our efforts on altering the triggers to his aggression and teaching better ways to deal with those triggers. Specifically, we wanted to make sure he had people to play with, and understood what people meant when they said he could not immediately join a game. We also wanted to make sure he was prepared for "questionable" calls at recess and could deal with these situations without fighting. The following shows what Kevin's plan looked like using each of the components of a good prevention plan: changing the trigger, teaching skills to deal with the triggers, rewards and losses, and biological and physical strategies.

CHANGE THE TRIGGERS

Since one of the main triggers was when peers said he could not play, we wanted to make this less likely to happen. We wanted to make sure he always had someone to play with. We were able to get the lunch aides to structure a game and make sure that Kevin was invited to play.

We also gave Kevin some games and balls to bring out to recess so other students would need to join him to play rather than Kevin having to join their ongoing activity.

Despite these efforts, there would still be triggers we could not stop. Occasionally Kevin might want to play a game that the lunch aides did not set up. In these instances a peer might tell Kevin that he could not play if the game was already in progress. So, he would have to learn to wait until a new game began, and not interpret the peer's refusal as a sign of rejection.

In addition, Kevin would still have to learn to deal with "questionable calls" during game play. Although we did steer him to play with peers less likely to argue, we could not ensure there would never be any arguments about questionable calls. Thus Kevin would have to learn how to deal with questionable calls without fighting.

TEACH SKILLS TO DEAL WITH THE TRIGGERS

I told Kevin that when peers said he could not play, it usually meant that he had to wait until the game was over. It did not mean that peers disliked him. I convinced him of this by reminding him that many of the same children who initially had not let him play, allowed him to play later when choosing up sides for a new game. We also discussed how he could find someone else to play with while he was waiting for the game he really wanted.

Then we talked about the issue of questionable calls at recess. I explained that he might be absolutely right about a call, but if he argues to the point of fighting, he will have less time to play at recess, both because he might have to sit out for fighting or simply because he wasted so much time arguing. I asked him what was more important, having more time at recess to play or having everyone agree that he is right about a call. He hesitantly agreed that he wanted more time to play. I suggested that if he did not argue when called "out" in a game like kickball or foursquare, then he could get back in the game sooner and have more time. I also reminded him that more children would want to play with him if he did not argue about the calls.

Both these skill lessons were summarized on a cue card. Whenever we teach skills, there is no guarantee that a child will use the skill in real

62

Cue Card

+ If kids say you cannot play, they mean to wait until the next game. It does not mean they dislike you. You can play another game while you are waiting.

+ There will be questionable calls. If you do not argue, you will have more time to play and more kids to play with.

life. In order to maximize the possibility that Kevin would really use the skills, we wanted to remind him of them just prior to the moment he needed them. His parents and I asked the teacher to review the cue card with Kevin just before recess every day for several weeks.

We also asked that one of the lunch aides try to do some live coaching with Kevin if she saw him getting upset about not getting to play, reminding him that he might just have to wait to play the next game. Similarly, she was asked to remind Kevin that he would have more time to play if he did not argue about a call, even though he might be right.

With the review of the cue card just prior to recess, and some live coaching of these skills at recess, Kevin did not show those aggressive behaviors at recess again.

TRY REWARD OR LOSS SYSTEMS

Kevin was aware that there would be consequences for aggression at recess, including loss of recess the next day and no TV at home. He was also offered rewards from his teacher for each day he went without a physical altercation, but he never asked about the reward. He seemed happy just to have made it through recess without any problems. Kevin had needed an education, not a reward program.

CONSIDER BIOLOGICAL AND PHYSICAL STRATEGIES

Kevin's parents had been told by several professionals in the school to consider medication to help him curb his aggression. His parents were considering this, but wanted to first give the prevention plan a chance. With the success of the prevention plan, Kevin's parents decided to hold off on medications.

With Kevin's better days at recess, he began to thrive. His grades improved and he made some solid friendships. His parents and his teachers were both relieved and felt better about their role in guiding Kevin.

The Four Types of Meltdown Situations

Now that we have explored how to create a general prevention plan and apply it to Kevin's difficulty, we can consider how we might apply the model to other situations. In my experience, most triggers for meltdowns can be grouped into one of the four categories below:

+ **Demands:** When children have to do a difficult task like schoolwork, a new social situation, or experience unpleasant sensory stimulation (such as trying a new food).

+ **Waiting:** When they do not get what they want immediately, or cannot get what they want at all, or have to stop doing something they like.

+ **Threats to self-image:** When situations cause children to feel ashamed or embarrassed, such as losing a game, making mistakes, being criticized, or getting teased.

+ **Unmet wishes for attention:** When others refuse to play or interact with them, when they are jealous of others, or when they fear being alone.

Chapters 7-10 show examples of prevention plans that were created for real children dealing with these types of situations. When we apply the general prevention plan to each of these more specific problem situations, some of the categories of intervention become more or less relevant. (For example, not every problem requires a reward or a loss program.) Using the general model presented in this chapter, we can tailor interventions to address the specific problem in each situation.

Chapter Summary

A good prevention plan has the following components:

+ **Change the triggers**. These might include changes to the:

  - *Sensory demand of the situation* (e.g., noise, light, touch, taste, smells).

  - *Timing of the situation* (e.g., avoiding tasks when a child is excessively hungry, tired, or sick).

  - *Task difficulty* (e.g., making a task easier or shorter in duration).

  - *Visual supports* (e.g., providing pictures or written words to explain what to do in a situation).

+ **Teach skills to deal with the triggers**. These are skills to replace the negative behaviors with positive, alternative ways to cope with the triggers.

+ **Try reward or loss systems**

  - Reward the positive alternative skills with praise, privileges, material rewards, or point systems that add up to larger rewards.

  - Loss systems should be used only if the triggering situation has been modified, the child knows a better way to deal with the situation, was reminded to engage in the positive behavior, but instead chose the disruptive behavior.

+ **Consider biological and physical strategies**, which might include:

  - Dietary changes

  - Exercise, meditation and other physical modes of relaxation

- When other interventions have failed and the behavior is severely interfering with functioning, we may want consult with a physician about the possibility of medication therapy.

PLANS FOR THE FOUR TYPES OF MELTDOWN SITUATIONS

7

DEMANDS

Problem behaviors are often triggered when children are told to do a difficult or unpleasant task. This might include doing schoolwork, eating certain foods, getting dressed, cleaning their rooms, or approaching a new social situation. The following pages provide plans to help children deal with some of these situations.

Do Your School Work

Jeff was a seven-year-old boy with mild reading and writing difficulties noted by his first grade teacher. Although the school did not see his difficulties as great enough to warrant special education services, he was behind the other students in his reading and spelling. In school, the teacher was able to keep him on task and Jeff tried hard to keep up with the rest of the class. But after school, homework time was a disaster. He resisted any reading and writing assignment, except for math, which he liked. His parents' attempts to have him read or write were met with silly jokes, falling to the floor, asking for snack, saying he was tired, or running all over the house. A five-minute worksheet could take an hour with his parents having to chase him around offering rewards or threatening punishment.

CHANGE THE TRIGGERS

To address his avoidance of homework, his parents first decided to focus on changing the triggers to his upset. Specifically, they tried to alter the timing and difficulty of his reading and writing homework. First they set a time to do homework soon after school, before he got too tired, and right after a snack, so he was not hungry. They made sure the area was quiet. They broke the homework down into smaller steps, initially just asking him to do one tiny part of it. Once started, he often was willing to do the other parts as well. They offered to read half the passages for him, letting him choose which he would read. Similarly, they only demanded that he write half the work, again letting him choose which he would write. Giving these choices ahead of time helped reduce his initial resistance significantly.

TEACH SKILLS TO DEAL WITH THE TRIGGERS

His parents explained that he was not supposed to be able to do all his work and it was expected that he would need help with it. The teacher confirmed this notion so that Jeff did not interpret his difficulty as a sign of failure but rather as an expected part of learning to do his homework.

His parents emphasized that he could always ask for help rather than avoid the work by pretending to be hungry or tired. They reviewed this skill just prior to doing homework each day.

The parents also arranged for private tutoring for his reading difficulties so that he could increase his ability and confidence to decode words. The tutor carefully planned her one-on-one lessons with fun work that he could easily do, building up to more challenging work later on. With her help, he became less intimidated with reading and thus more willing to approach homework.

TRY REWARD OR LOSS SYSTEMS

His parents reminded him that he had to do homework before watching TV or playtime. This daily immediate reward was more powerful for Jeff than any promise of long-term rewards (like buying new games or special privileges).

CONSIDER BIOLOGICAL AND PHYSICAL STRATEGIES

One interesting thing they noted was that on days when he had exercised outside, he was more willing to attempt the work. Thus his parents tried to schedule time for exercise each day.

With more choice over assignments, tutoring for reading, and greater willingness to accept help without seeing it as a sign of failure, Jeff consistently cooperated with homework time. The following quick reference guide lists many ideas from which to choose in designing a plan to help your child do school work.

Quick Reference Guide for Problems Doing School Work

CHANGE THE TRIGGERS

+ **Sensory stimulation**

  – Noise: provide quieter areas to work with fewer students surrounding the child.

  – Light: consider incandescent versus fluorescent light, as many children are distracted by the flickering of fluorescent lights.

  – Smells: reduce smells in work area

  – Touch: some students might require further space from other children, as even accidental touching from other students can be distracting. Other children might attend better with some opportunity for certain tactile feedback. For example, some children concentrate better when sitting on special cushions, or fidgeting with objects of certain texture. Keep in mind that some children attend *worse* when fidgeting with objects, so you must decide what's best for *your* child.

+ **Timing of the situation.** Avoid giving work to students when they are overly hungry, or before bed, when they are tired. Students may need a snack, physical activity, or a rest before work.

+ **Task difficulty** (simplify the work)

  – When possible, give the student a *choice* of what work to do (e.g., choosing which book to read or what story to write).

  – Similarly, use the *child's interests* to make the assignment more engaging. Allow a child to write, talk about, or present a special interest. Or make math or language arts assignments related to special interests. For example, a child who likes dinosaurs could do math problems about the age or size of dinosaurs, or write sentences about dinosaurs for language arts.

- *Break down larger assignments* into smaller increments and ask the child to just do a smaller part of it to begin.

- Change recall tasks into *multiple-choice* tasks. For example, instead of asking a student to write about what she did over the summer (where she has to recall what she did), describe several things she did over the summer and let her choose which she wants to write about.

- Children who have *difficulties with handwriting* should be allowed to write less, dictate to tapes or a scribe (a person assigned to write for them), or use keyboarding (alpha-smarts or computers) to reduce the challenge. Sometimes asking a child to just say out loud what she will write helps her get started with a writing task.

- *Shorten the time* children must engage in a difficult task. For example, one can reduce the amount of homework, or the amount of time spent engaged in a difficult class assignment.

- Give *extra time on tasks* such as tests, so the child does not have to rush or be distracted by worries about running out of time.

- Allow the child to *change the medium* of an assignment. For example, a writing project could be turned into a film, oral presentation or a slide show.

- Ask the child to *repeat instructions* before engaging in the task to see what she did or did not understand.

+ **Visual supports**

- *Use graphic organizers.* These are visual maps that summarize information in a web format to aid in comprehension and later recall. For example, a child might be helped to summarize the main points of a story and show with arrows how different ideas are connected. The web can be used to aid in understanding how the ideas relate to each other and help the student recall the information later to write or talk about the topic (see sample below).

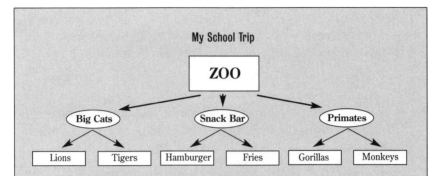

- *Use a cue card or checklist* to summarize the steps needed to perform a particular task, like doing a math problem or writing task, rather than relying on verbal instructions alone.

TEACH SKILLS TO DEAL WITH THE TRIGGERS

+ **Explain to students that they are not expected to know what to do** when they attempt new work. Challenge them to see how long they can tolerate not knowing what to do. Can they wait for one minute, five minutes, or long enough to stay with the task until they can figure out what to do?

+ **Teach them the following steps for trying difficult work:**
  - Try it first.
  - Ask for help or watch someone else do it first.
  - Break it down into smaller steps.
  - Make a deal: do one part and ask for help with the other part.
  - Ask for a quick break if needed and come back and try again.

TRY REWARD OR LOSS SYSTEMS

+ **Make access to playtime contingent on cooperating with work.** For each bit of work attempted or completed, give rewards or points that can be exchanged for rewards, like time playing games. (Note: Regular play and exercise may be crucial to ready a child to do work, so we do not want to limit *all* play until work is completed.)

+ **Loss systems should be used only if the child was reminded** just before the work that he could ask for help or take a brief break. If instead he acts aggressively and refuses to try the work, one can withhold rewards or privileges.

CONSIDER BIOLOGICAL AND PHYSICAL STRATEGIES

+ **Regular exercise** has been shown to increase students' attention and learning over time.

+ **Omega-3 supplements** may improve attention and concentration on academic tasks, though their effects may not be immediate (Sinn & Bryan, 2007). Students with ADHD who take medication may discover that they also benefit from taking the medication after school to help complete homework. Since stimulants can cause insomnia, doses need to be adjusted so that the effects wear off before bedtime.

Try It. It's Delicious.

Sandy was a six-year-old girl who refused to eat anything but Goldfish crackers. Her mother tried to get her to eat some other foods, such as cheese, chicken nuggets, and some fruits and vegetables. The more she pushed Sandy to do it, the more Sandy resisted. There are few things little kids can control about their lives, but eating is one of them. Sandy and her parents were in a power struggle. They tried rewarding Sandy with movies and toys for trying other foods, which sometimes worked, but as soon as Sandy sensed their excitement that she would try another food, she refused once again.

Alternatively, they tried to withhold the Goldfish crackers until she would eat something else, which would result in screaming tantrums that lasted hours. Although this might have eventually worked, the parents were not willing to follow through with withholding food indefinitely until she would try something else. This is understandable since, unlike most kids who might "give in" after several hours, Sandy could go a whole day without eating unless given the crackers.

In tracking the ABCs of this behavior, it seemed not to matter who asked her to eat; she would avoid all other foods but Goldfish crackers. She often succeeded in this avoidance, because her parents would eventually give in and give her the crackers. Although intervention could focus only on withholding the crackers until she ate something else, her parents were not up for this challenge. Instead, treatment focused on ways to gradually expose her to other foods with lots of incentives for trying them.

CHANGE THE TRIGGERS

Since control seemed so central to Sandy's difficulties, she was always given choices about what foods to try. The parents began by assessing her special interests. She loved dinosaurs. They were able to find dinosaur-shaped crackers, pasta and chicken nuggets. They also found a cookie cutter shaped like a dinosaur, which could be used to shape pieces of apple and pears. The first new food they introduced was the dinosaur crackers. Picking a food closest to what she already ate made the transition to new foods easier.

Using these special interests, her parents gradually exposed her to the new foods by asking her first just to look at the foods. Next she was asked to smell them, taste them, and then eventually eat a small piece.

In addition, her parents persuaded several of her closest friends to eat those items in front of her, modeling how good they tasted. She often wanted to be like some of her best friends, and this was a powerful way to bait her interest in trying the foods.

TEACH SKILLS TO DEAL WITH THE TRIGGERS

The treatment of choice for most "fears" is gradual exposure to the feared item. To get Sandy to gradually look at, smell, taste and then eat new foods, they explained to her how taking these small steps to trying new things helps people get over their fears. Sandy was reminded of the many times she feared something until she tried it, and then found it to be okay afterward.

TRY REWARD OR LOSS SYSTEMS

Sandy was given quarters for each time she looked, smelled, tasted or ate a bit of new food. These quarters could be saved for a trip to the local toy store.

All along, the parents took a neutral attitude so as to avoid getting into a power struggle. Although Goldfish crackers were not readily available when she was trying new foods, they also were not forbidden. To forbid the crackers might remind Sandy of past power struggles and increase her resistance. Sandy did not initially eat a new food, but was usually willing to at least look at it. As she earned quarters, she was willing to take a chance and smell, taste and eventually eat the food. Once she had tried an item twice, it seemed to become part of the list of foods she would eat. Most phobias work this way, once exposed to the item and finding nothing bad happens, the fear subsides. This was the case for Sandy. After two weeks of doing this once per day, her circle of foods had widened to eating pastas, fruits, and chicken nuggets. In addition, she began to spontaneously try new foods in restaurants and other places as well.

Quick Reference Guide for Problems Avoiding New Foods

CHANGE THE TRIGGERS

+ **Sensory stimulation**

  - Noise and light: consider quieter areas to try new foods to avoid sensory overload.

  - Smells: pick foods with smells similar to that of her favored foods, or gradually introduce foods with new smells.

  - Touch: pick foods with textures similar to that of her favored food. For example, a child who only likes macaroni could try other pastas before moving on to other textures.

  - Taste: introduce new foods that have tastes similar to that of her favored foods, or begin with sweet items (even candy) to allow the child to be open to trying new things.

+ **Timing of the situation.** It is best to try new foods when both adult and child are not rushed and not otherwise too stressed. If mealtimes are usually stressful, with preparation and getting kids to sit down, this may not be the ideal time.

+ **Task difficulty**

  - Give the child a *choice* of foods to eat.

  - Instead of asking children to eat a large piece of food, *create a hierarchy of difficulty* from looking at the food, to smelling it, to licking it, to chewing a small piece, and then to swallowing some.

  - *Use the child's interests* to make the food more appealing. If they like certain animals, make the food look like the animals.

  - *Use the child's role models* or friends to model eating the new foods. For example, if the child likes a superhero, explain how the superhero eats that food.

+ **Visual supports.** Remind the child verbally and with cue cards or posters that she does not have to eat everything, just look, smell, taste, chew, or swallow a little bit. Show her the rewards that await her when she tries the foods.

TEACH SKILLS TO DEAL WITH THE TRIGGERS

+ **Think about what the child likes to do** and explain that eating certain foods will give her the strength and ability to do those things (e.g., sports, reading, dancing, etc).

+ **Show the child the effects** that those foods have on her role models and good friends. For example, explain how her favorite singer or best friend eats a particularly healthy food.

+ **Explain to the child the way fear works.**

  – There are true fears and false alarms. True fears keep us away from things that are actually dangerous, such as being afraid to run out in traffic. False alarms keep us away from things that are actually good for us, such as being afraid of healthy food.

  – With false alarms, we usually fear the thing until we try it. Once we try it, it turns out to be much better than we thought. Remind her of times when she was afraid of something that was harmless and then it turned out to be okay after she tried it.

  – Then help her gradually face her fear by looking, smelling, tasting and then eating the new foods.

TRY REWARD OR LOSS SYSTEMS

+ **For each step of trying a new food, offer a reward.** Rewards can include preferred foods, toys, or privileges, or points that add up to buy those things. Make sure you also provide the intrinsic reward that they are now eating something healthy and have conquered their fear.

+ **Loss systems can be limited** to withholding access to favored foods until new foods are looked at, smelled, tasted, chewed or swallowed.

CONSIDER BIOLOGICAL AND PHYSICAL STRATEGIES

+ **Allowing a child to get hungry can improve the possibility that they will try a new food.** (Though if they are overly hungry, they may be more prone to melt down.)

+ **Exercise just prior to trying a new food can increase appetite.** In general, exercise can reduce anxiety, increase mood, and therefore increase willingness to try new things.

Hurry Up, the Bus is Coming!

Jared was nine years old and had a hard time getting ready for school in the morning. His parents found it hard to wake him. Once awake, he stayed in bed unless they continually told him to get up. He was completely capable of dressing himself, brushing his teeth and getting his own breakfast, but he did none of these things without constant reminding from his parents. He did all these things for himself on the weekends, but during the week, he did them so slowly that his parents helped him through most of these routines to get him to the bus on time. He seemed to get distracted by looking out the window, looking over his games, debating over what clothes to wear or what to eat for breakfast, and sometimes just generally spacing out.

On many days, his parents, who were also rushing to get themselves ready, had raised their voices at Jared to move him along resulting in Jared becoming upset and taking longer. This led to a downward spiral with Jared and his parents getting increasingly angry. The ABCs of this behavior showed that school days were always worse than weekends. Jared had also commented that he did not like school, thus we could infer that part of his delay was related to his desire to avoid going to school. His parents' angry reactions when he dawdled seemed to trigger further delay from him.

We concluded that his behavior was motivated to avoid these stressful morning routines when the eventual outcome was having to go to school. If instead he could look forward to a more fun activity, then he might be more motivated, as he was on the weekends.

CHANGE THE TRIGGERS

To intervene, we began by identifying fun activities that Jared could do if he finished his morning routine early enough on schooldays. These included playing video games, watching TV, and exercising with his dad. To do these activities, he would have to get up a little earlier, and thus get to bed earlier the night before. His parents also picked out clothes and breakfast items the night before, so everything would be ready to go in the morning. To help Jared wake up once he was out of bed, they did some jumping jacks and sit-ups with him, which were activities he enjoyed.

TEACH SKILLS TO DEAL WITH THE TRIGGERS

They explained to him that if he could get dressed and eat by a certain hour, they would let him play with his video games, watch TV, or exercise with Dad. Since he had never been able to do these things on weekday mornings, he was motivated to work hard to have this extra time.

TRY REWARD OR LOSS SYSTEMS

The rewards and losses were built right into the skill lesson. Getting ready early resulted in extra privileges. If he decided to play with his games before he was ready, those items were removed from him until he had completed his morning routine.

Despite a couple of late nights that led to some difficult mornings, the parents reported that the morning routine was no longer the struggle it had been. He independently got himself dressed and ready and commented how much he liked the time to play in the morning before a hard day of school.

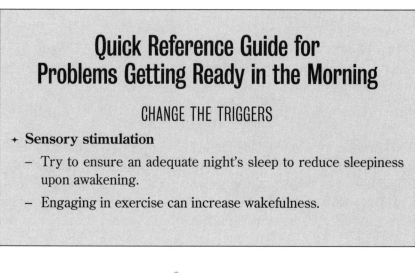

Quick Reference Guide for Problems Getting Ready in the Morning

CHANGE THE TRIGGERS

+ **Sensory stimulation**
  - Try to ensure an adequate night's sleep to reduce sleepiness upon awakening.
  - Engaging in exercise can increase wakefulness.

- Noise and light: Bright lights and gradually increasing noise level can help arouse a sleepy child.

- Smells and taste: delicious smelling foods can also motivate a child to get up and come to breakfast.

- Touch: Certain types of touch, hugs, and even playful wrestling can increase wakefulness.

+ **Timing of the situation.** If the child has had adequate sleep, it's best to start the routine as early as possible so there is less rush, and possibly time for rewarding activities when the morning routine is finished.

+ **Task difficulty.** To reduce the stress of the morning, try to do as much as possible the night before. For example, bathe, choose clothes and breakfast items, pack lunch, get school bag packed, and have toothbrush out with toothpaste ready to go before going to bed.

+ **Visual supports.** Use a morning checklist to remind the child what to do and what reward might be waiting for him when done (e.g., "Wash face, brush teeth, put on clothes, come to breakfast, and when you're done, you can play games"). Try pointing to the checklist rather than just verbally reminding the child what to do, as it is often met with less resistance.

TEACH SKILLS TO DEAL WITH THE TRIGGERS

+ **Explain** to him that the morning routine can be hard if he is tired, and together agree on what things to do to help him be less tired, like getting to bed earlier, exercising in the morning, and getting things ready the night before.

+ **Teach him what is in it for him** when he can get through the morning routine more quickly. Highlight the preferred activities he will have time for when he is done with his morning routine.

TRY REWARD OR LOSS SYSTEMS

+ **Give access to preferred activities** like games, books, TV, playing outside, or going for a walk with a parent for getting done with the morning routine more quickly.

+ **If a child sneaks access to a toy or game without permission** before he is done with his morning routine, you can consider removing access to that toy or game for a brief period of time (e.g., 24 hours). Withholding toys or privileges for longer periods of time often worsens the situation by decreasing the child's motivation.

CONSIDER BIOLOGICAL AND PHYSICAL STRATEGIES

+ **Exercise in the morning** can help arouse the mind and body.

+ **Medications should be a last resort** when other strategies have failed. Melatonin may be an effective supplement to promote a good night's sleep in children (Pavonen, Nieminen-VanWendt et al., 2003) so they can awake more easily in the morning. Stimulants can help those with ADHD focus better in the mornings to get through their routine, but these medications often take about thirty minutes before they begin to take effect.

Clean Up

Eve was a bright but messy, eleven-year-old girl who continually left her belongings all over the house. Her parents' efforts to enforce the rule to clean up after herself were not successful as Eve always said she had something else to do. They offered her rewards (a video, snacks, staying up later) for cleaning up, but she still stalled. Then, later that evening or the next day, she might put away a fraction of what she left out and then ask for her reward. Her parents would usually give her the reward since she had at least done something, even if it was a day late.

When Eve completely refused to clean up a mess that was in everyone's way, her parents explained that if they had to clean it up, they would take the toys away from her. At this point she would begin to hit herself in the head. This behavior was alarming to the parents and would result in their holding her and telling her the dangers of this kind of action. After Eve calmed down in their arms, they often forgot that they were going to take the toy from her. Instead, they had cleaned up her toys for her, and continued to give her access to the toys later.

The ABCs of these behaviors showed that Eve was successful in avoiding cleaning up. Her stalling behavior and hitting herself were ultimately effective in helping her avoid cleaning up. Although it was clear that her parents had to stop rewarding Eve's avoidance, it was not clear why Eve went to such an extent to avoid cleaning up in the first place. A good prevention plan should consider how to make cleaning up less challenging in addition to making Eve more responsible for cleaning up her mess.

CHANGE THE TRIGGERS

We decided to make it easier for Eve to clean up by purchasing containers with labels for all her toys so it would be easier for her to know where to put them. Second, we suggested that her parents initially offer to help her clean up so Eve did not feel overwhelmed by the amount of work involved. We also asked them to hold off from asking her to clean up just before bed or at other times when Eve was tired.

TEACH SKILLS TO DEAL WITH THE TRIGGERS
AND TRY REWARD OR LOSS SYSTEMS

We also taught Eve that she must comply the first time in order to get her reward for cleaning up. No reward was giving for "eventually" cleaning up. In addition, we explained that if she refused to participate in cleaning up, then her parents would remove the items and they would be off limits to her for 24 hours. If she hit herself, her parents were told to ignore it. If they were concerned that she might really hurt herself, they could hold her, but they could not agree to give the toys back before the 24 hours had elapsed.

Although Eve continued to stall at first, after a week she was much more willing to clean up given the ease of the task with organized containers and her parents' help. She did refuse one day, and when told she would lose her toys, she did hit herself. Yet after seeing that this did not get her toys back or get much of a reaction from her parents, she did not do it again. Both Eve and her parents reported feeling less stress and more confident in themselves.

Quick Reference Guide
for Problems Cleaning Up

CHANGE THE TRIGGERS

+ **Sensory stimulation.** Clean-up time will go best when the child is not overwhelmed. Competing sources of stimulation like TV or games should be stopped before attempting to clean up.

+ **Timing of the situation.** Consider when you ask children to clean up. Try to avoid just before bed when they may be overtired.

+ **Task difficulty**
  – Offer to help clean up by sharing in the work or helping them get started.

– Create labeled bins to make cleaning up and finding toys easier.

+ **Visual supports.** Consider how clear the instructions are to clean up. Does the child know where things go? Use written or picture labels to make it clearer.

TEACH SKILLS TO DEAL WITH THE TRIGGERS

+ **Teach ways to organize belongings.** Children will find things better when they keep things organized in drawers or bins.

+ **Explain that you can trust them to play with certain items** only if they can clean them up. If they don't, they may lose the privilege of playing with those items.

TRY REWARD OR LOSS SYSTEMS

+ **Consider using rewards for cleaning up,** such as an allowance, access to certain activities, toys, time with parents, snacks, or points towards long-term rewards (i.e., items that you might buy at the end of an entire week of successfully cleaning up).

+ **If a child refuses to clean up items** and parents end up cleaning up, consider limiting access to those items for brief periods (e.g., 24 hours).

Let's Go to the Party

Carrie was a five-year-old girl who had always been shy around new people and reticent to explore new situations on her own. When she was invited to birthday parties, she would go only if her parents stayed with her and, even then, she would not participate in any of the activities, choosing instead to cling to her parents. If they demanded that she try an activity, then she would whine and eventually scream or hit her parents.

When her parents wanted her to go to a children's party or recreation activity she often refused to go. If the family tried to take her, she would fall to the floor and refuse to leave. Her parents had tried gentle encouragement and sometimes physically dragging her out. Neither had changed her level of cooperation. Usually, once she was at the new place for over an hour, she would begin to warm up and enjoy herself.

Despite her eventual accommodation to these new situations, she continued to battle her parents before such outings. Her parents began to feel like hostages to their daughter's anxiety.

CHANGE THE TRIGGERS AND
TEACH SKILLS TO DEAL WITH THE TRIGGERS

On my advice, her parents reassured her that she did not have to fully participate in new activities, but could instead stay by her parents' side and watch until she felt more comfortable. This approach was supportive of her "slow to warm up" temperament and avoided power struggles, yet continued to help her face her fears. Her parents also said that she could bring her teddy bear with her for comfort until she felt better.

We taught Carrie that, although she is often nervous for the first hour of going anywhere, she usually felt better after that. She was reminded of all the times she had been initially fearful and then later enjoyed herself. She was asked to predict how long it would take for her to feel comfortable in each new situation. The question itself helped her to understand that her anxiety was only temporary.

TRY REWARD OR LOSS SYSTEMS

A reward system was also set up to provide incentives to Carrie for going out or attending parties, without the demand that she participate fully. Once there, if she did not participate after the normal warm-up period, they would offer more incentives for trying an activity. For example, at a birthday party, her parents might offer her a special snack if she would participate in a game the kids were playing. Her parents would begin the game with her if she would not do it alone and then, once she was enjoying it, they would watch from afar.

As Carrie and her parents continued to use this approach and went out regularly, Carrie gained more insight into the way her anxiety worked. By reviewing each outing with her, she learned that she did need time to warm up, but then would be okay later. She even commented to her parents, "You know it takes me an hour until I am comfortable." With both Carrie and her parents accepting and working with her warm-up period, there was much less conflict and more willingness on her part to go out.

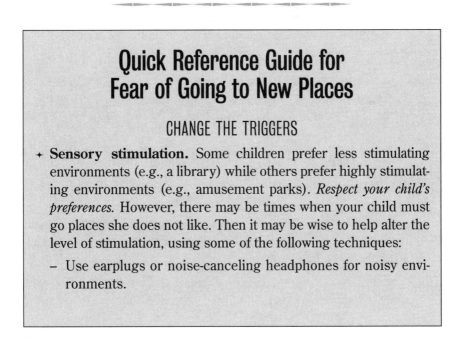

Quick Reference Guide for Fear of Going to New Places

CHANGE THE TRIGGERS

+ **Sensory stimulation.** Some children prefer less stimulating environments (e.g., a library) while others prefer highly stimulating environments (e.g., amusement parks). *Respect your child's preferences.* However, there may be times when your child must go places she does not like. Then it may be wise to help alter the level of stimulation, using some of the following techniques:

  – Use earplugs or noise-canceling headphones for noisy environments.

- Offer frequent breaks in quieter areas for crowded places. For example, take a walk outside during an indoor birthday party to get a break from the crowd or noise.

- Allow the child to use a favorite stuffed animal, toy, or game to keep occupied and soothed during the outing.

+ **Timing of the situation.** Try to time your outings when the child is not exhausted or overly hungry. Consider bringing snacks or allowing her to rest in the car before attempting a challenging outing.

+ **Task difficulty**

- *Break down the feared situation into smaller steps*, such as allowing her to start by watching the event while staying close to parents, then trying one minute of the activity and so on. Allow the child to choose what step she wants to face. Often, allowing the child to watch others take part in an activity without forcing her to join in allows her to eventually participate without resistance.

- Allow the child to *take breaks* during the outing or reduce the total time she needs to stay in the new place by arriving late or leaving early.

+ **Visual supports.** Use a written schedule to explain to the child what is going to happen at the outing. Similarly, go over any instructions for the games that might be played if the outing is a social event.

TEACH SKILLS TO DEAL WITH THE TRIGGERS

+ **Explain how fears work.**

- There are "true fears" and "false alarms." True fears keep us away from things that are actually dangerous, such as being afraid to run out in traffic. False alarms keep us away from things that are actually good for us or potentially enjoyable.

- With false alarms, we fear the situation until we try it. Once we try it, we realize it is much better or easier than we thought it would be. Remind the child of times when she was afraid of something that was harmless and then it turned out to be okay after she tried it.

– Help the child develop a hierarchy of facing the feared situation, from just talking about the event, to watching the event, to fully participating in the event. Ask what part the child feels up to trying, and then explain that once she is comfortable, she can move up the hierarchy to the next situation. Give her a sense that she can control when she will go to the next level, yet continue to encourage her to try the next step.

TRY REWARD OR LOSS SYSTEMS

+ **Use incentives** such as snacks, toys, privileges, or points that can be exchanged for rewards for trying to face each step of a challenging situation.

+ **Avoid punishing children for their anxious feelings.** Instead, continue to encourage them to take small steps towards facing the fear.

CONSIDER BIOLOGICAL AND PHYSICAL STRATEGIES

+ **Try using relaxation activities** such as deep breathing, meditation, or stretching to help calm the youngster before facing their fear.

+ **Vigorous exercise can greatly reduce anxiety temporarily.** Thus, consider morning exercise on the day of an outing.

+ **Medication should be a last resort.** If the interventions above have failed, and the behavior is severely limiting where the child can go, it would be wise to seek professional help, including the possibility of a medication evaluation. Sometimes, anti-anxiety and anti-depressant medications can help children to expose themselves to the feared situation, reducing fear over time and ultimately allowing the medications to be faded out.

8

WAITING

Most children have some difficulty waiting for what they want. The following describes three of the most common situations in which children must delay getting their way. The most straightforward example is when children see or think of something they want, which they actually can have, yet they will just have to wait some period of time. Another situation is when children can't have something at all, a situation we call "accepting no for an answer." A related situation is when children must stop doing something fun, such as playing, to do something less fun, like doing homework. All these situations require children to delay their gratification. When this delay is imposed, some children melt down or tantrum.

Just Wait

Ian was five years old and attended Kindergarten. His teachers complained that he constantly wanted their attention. When the teachers were helping other students or trying to read a story, Ian would interrupt to ask a question or simply chat with the teachers about his day or weekend. The teachers would tell him to wait, but he would do it again just a minute later.

At home, Ian's parents also complained that he interrupted discussions with other grown-ups, interfered with their phone calls, and could not tolerate it when they were talking with his four-year-old sister. In general, they described Ian as a high-energy child who wanted constant attention from others. When Ian had to wait to get his parents attention, he would get angry and yell or begin hitting them to get them to look at him.

The ABCs of his angry hitting behavior showed that waiting for adult attention was usually the trigger. His yelling and hitting often succeeded in getting adult attention, even though it was angry attention. His parents wanted to help him learn to wait.

CHANGE THE TRIGGERS

To help Ian deal with waiting, I asked his parents and teacher to create brief times for him when he could have their undivided adult attention if he waited patiently without interrupting. In school, the teacher gave him two five-minute periods to chat exclusively with her. At home, he was scheduled to get a "special time" with a parent each night for twenty minutes when they would talk with him or play exclusively with him.

Both the parents and teachers then used a "traffic light" system to show him visually when it was or was not okay to approach them at other times. The parents hung a green or red piece of paper in the kitchen to indicate when he could or could not interrupt, and the teacher used a similar red/green paper to tell the class when it was or was not okay to interrupt. To help him understand the passage of time so he could know when his special talk time was coming, his parents and teacher used a

94

visual timer (like a kitchen timer with a large colored shape that shrinks as time passes—available at most special education stores and websites).

We also gave Ian a set of activities he could do independently when he was waiting for his teacher or parents. Since he was a high-energy kid in need of lots of stimulation, we gave him puzzles, games, drawing materials, and other activities in a "to do" box to help him occupy himself in school and at home while he was waiting.

TEACH SKILLS TO DEAL WITH THE TRIGGERS

We taught him the times it was okay to interrupt (when the adults were not talking to others) and how to wait for a pause and say "excuse me." The green and red signs were also introduced to remind him if it was an okay time to interrupt.

We described how he could occupy himself with the "to do" box while he was waiting, and explained that even when adults were not talking with him, they were still thinking about him and proud of him for playing independently.

Finally, we taught him about the "invisible reward" for waiting patiently: that adults will be so happy they will give him more of what he wants later (i.e., their undivided attention).

TRY REWARD OR LOSS SYSTEMS

The most important reward was to praise him for playing independently and waiting. Before he had a chance to interrupt (about a one-minute interval), the teacher and his parents would comment on how proud they were that he was not interrupting. Eventually they were able to increase the interval to about twenty minutes before praising him for not interrupting. Finally, for waiting patiently, Ian would earn a special one-on-one time with his teacher or parent. Since he craved attention, this positive praise was very meaningful to him.

If Ian interrupted when he was not allowed (when the red card was up), teachers and parents were told to say only one thing: to remind him of when he would be able to talk with them. After they made this statement, they would ignore him until his time came or the green card was up. This was more helpful than totally ignoring him, which had previously led Ian to think he would never get to talk with the adult, which had increased his frustration.

Although Ian continued to be an active and talkative young boy, he quickly learned to occupy himself when adults were unavailable. In addition, he was able to wait for his time with the adults using the timers. Both the teacher and his parents agreed that Ian was much less needy and more patient.

Quick Reference Guide for Problems Waiting

CHANGE THE TRIGGERS

+ **Sensory stimulation.** Many children who have trouble waiting require lots of stimulation. It is the lack of stimulation that leads to boredom and difficulty waiting. Thus, it is crucial that these children have engaging activities to do while waiting. Examples might include:

  - A "to do" box that has several activities from which to pick

  - Access to favored games or activities, such as books, hand-held video games, or DVD players to help them pass the time while waiting

  - Some job to do, such as helping their parents find items in a store rather than just waiting for their parent to be done with shopping

+ **Timing of the situation.** Children will have greater ability to wait when they are not overly tired. If hungry, they will have more difficulty waiting for food. Thus, these may not be the times to work on waiting.

+ **Task difficulty**

  - *Schedule times* when they can have what they want. Knowing they will be able to get what they want at a specified time can make it easier to wait.

  - *Keep them busy* with activities to occupy themselves while waiting (as described above).

  - *They can write or draw their questions* for parents or teachers so they will not forget what they wanted to say while waiting.

+ **Visual supports**

  - Use a *visual timer* (timer or clock) to help children know when they will be able to get what they want. Many specialty timers exist that look like traditional kitchen timers, yet have a large colored area that shrinks as the time passes. This helps children appreciate how much time is left.

  - Use *red and green cards* (like a traffic light) to indicate when a child may or may not ask for what he wants.

  - Explain that a *closed door* can indicate not to interrupt, or at least to knock before entering.

  - Use a *written schedule* to indicate when the child will get what he or she wants.

TEACH SKILLS TO DEAL WITH THE TRIGGERS

+ **Explain the hidden payoff of waiting.** "Others will be happy when you wait and they'll be more likely to give you what you want." This can be highlighted by offering greater amounts of what they want for waiting longer periods of time, so that children can clearly see the benefit of waiting. For example, a child who wants a snack can learn that he can have one piece if he waits a minute, or two pieces if he waits five minutes, or three pieces if he waits fifteen minutes.

+ **Teach the rules for interrupting.**

 – In classrooms, raise your hand and wait to be called on. In conversation, wait for a pause, or when other are not busy.

 – Try to get into the person's line of vision so they see you.

 – Say "excuse me," and then ask for what you want.

 – Consider how many times one can interrupt. For example, sometimes students are told they can interrupt only two times in a class period, then they have to wait until the next period.

TRY REWARD OR LOSS SYSTEMS

+ **Praise children for waiting without interrupting.** Consider using a point system for each time a child waits. You may have to praise him for waiting very short periods of time at first (e.g., under a minute) and then extend the interval for longer periods of time. If you wait too long, he may interrupt and you will lose your chance to praise him for the time he did wait.

+ **When interrupted, remind the child to wait** until the specified time, and then ignore further interruptions.

CONSIDER BIOLOGICAL AND PHYSICAL STRATEGIES

+ **Vigorous exercise can temporarily improve mood and self-control,** and thus may increase the ability to wait.

+ **Medications can be useful, but should be a last resort.** When the above interventions have failed, and difficulty waiting exists across many situations, severely limiting the child's ability to function at home or in school, then an evaluation by a qualified mental health professional should be pursued and the possibility of medication may be considered.

You Can't Always Get What You Want

Jamie was a ten-year-old living with his parents and two younger siblings. For several years, his parents had tried to avoid taking him out to toy stores, restaurants, or the grocery store because he would always beg them for a new game, toy, candy, or dessert and make a scene by crying and cursing at them when he did not get his way. Although they had on occasion given in when they were in a rush, usually they did not. Rather, they just waited out the tantrum.

Although he was always impatient, the problem had worsened with the arrival of his then five- and two-year-old siblings with whom he had to share his parents' attention and household resources. When Jamie began to tantrum to get something, his brothers would imitate him and demand to have what they wanted, too. His parents were feeling overwhelmed by their children's demands. They found it easier to ignore the demands at home, but when they were out in public, they were embarrassed by their children's behavior. They felt unable to go anywhere without someone losing control.

The ABCs suggested that going out with all the kids was more of a trigger than going just with Jamie. Jamie knew that his parents could not cope with his demands as easily when his siblings went along and, in fact, his parents gave in to his demands more often when all the kids were together. In addition, Jamie had commented about his brothers getting "everything," suggesting some jealousy of them. His parents had punished Jamie for tantrumming by refusing to take him out again, yet this had not altered his behavior. The next outing he would have just as many demands and tantrums if he did not get what he wanted.

CHANGE THE TRIGGERS

Given Jamie's comments, we hypothesized that his demands were in part related to feeling jealous of the attention his brothers received. So we made sure Jamie regularly got a special time with his parents without his brothers. For twenty minutes each night, one of his parents would play with him alone.

Because going out with all the boys was especially challenging, his parents and I decided to limit outings with Jamie to those times when his brothers did not have to accompany them. Additionally, his parents tried to avoid taking him to the most tempting places (e.g., a toy store or near a candy shop). They also gave him a set of activities (books, magazines, or hand-held video game) to occupy himself when on an outing so that his demands did not arise out of boredom.

TEACH SKILLS TO DEAL WITH THE TRIGGERS

I had Jamie's parents remind him before he went out about what would happen if he could "accept no" for an answer or not even ask them for something. They explained that they would be so pleased that they would give him something else he wanted at the end of the outing. The things they chose to give him were not "extra" rewards, but things they would have given him anyway, like some alone time with Dad, time to watch a show on TV or play outside, dessert after dinner, or a small snack.

To practice this skill, we first prompted him to ask for things we knew he did not want, like asking for a snack right after eating. We would say no and prompt him to say "okay" without getting mad. Then we would say, "That was great! You accepted no, which makes us so happy that we will give you something else you want later." His parents tried to build up a history of praising him for accepting no before taking him on outings outside the home. On the way to an outing they would remind him how well he had done with "accepting no" and that they were confident he could do it on the outing as well so he could make his parents proud and get something else he wanted later.

TRY REWARD OR LOSS SYSTEMS

Built into the skill of "accepting no" was the reward of getting something else later. Usually these were privileges that Jamie would have received anyway, but his parents emphasized the fact that he would receive these things for accepting no. In addition, his parents put him on a point system, giving him a point every time he accepted no or did not ask for something on an outing (one point per outing). At the end of the week, those points could be exchanged for a special reward, such as a new toy, game, or special trip on the weekend.

His parents also continued to use consequences for tantrums on outings, which meant he could not go along on the next scheduled outing and he might lose access to his video games or TV at home that night.

Over time it was clear that Jamie appreciated the time alone with his parents, often commenting how nice it was to just be with them. As he became more aware of the importance of "accepting no" when requesting material items, he seemed less focused on getting those things as he asked much less often. His parents appreciated the change in Jamie's behavior and were pleased to make the effort to spend more time with him. The parents commented that perhaps Jamie's previous insatiable desire for toys was partially a substitute for his wish to be with them.

Quick Reference Guide for Problems "Accepting No"

CHANGE THE TRIGGERS

+ **Sensory stimulation.** Many children who have trouble waiting require a lot of stimulation. It is lack of stimulation that can lead to boredom and subsequent asking for things to entertain themselves. Thus it is crucial that these children have engaging activities to do while waiting. Examples might include:

  - A "to do" box that has several activities from which to pick

  - Access to favored games or activities, like books, handheld video games or DVD players to help them pass the time while waiting

  - Some job to do, like helping their parents find items in a store rather than just waiting for them to be done with shopping

+ **Timing of the situation.** Children will have greater ability to accept no when they are not overly tired or hungry.

✦ Task difficulty

– *Schedule times* when they can have something they want if they accept no or refrain from asking for things. Knowing they will be able to get something else they want gives them a reason to control themselves.

– *Keep them busy* with activities to occupy themselves while waiting (as described above).

– *Reduce temptations* by avoiding outings and areas in which they will be exposed to highly preferred items that they cannot have. For example, avoid taking them to a toy store to buy something for another child unless you are also buying for them.

✦ Visual supports

– Use a visual cue to prime them for *what they will get* if they accept no or do not ask for things. These might be pictures of regularly scheduled fun activities or access to toys, games, or snacks (such a picture sequence is depicted in "accepting no for an answer" in the *Social Skills Picture Book*, Baker, 2001).

– Use a *visual timer* (digital or color-coded timer) to help children know when they will be able to get something else that they want.

– Use a *written schedule* to indicate when the child will get something he wants.

TEACH SKILLS TO DEAL WITH THE TRIGGERS

✦ **Explain the hidden payoff of accepting no:** "that others will be happy and want to give you something else you want later." Just saying no to youngsters who have difficulty problem solving can seem like the end of the world. Knowing that something else they want is in store for them can give them a reason to maintain self-control. To practice "accepting no":

- Begin with items the child does not really want. Have him ask for something and then say no. Prompt the child to say "okay" and not get mad. Praise him for accepting no and then offer another preferred item or privilege later because he accepted no.

- Prime him before situations in which you might have to say no to something he really wants. Tell him if he calmly accepts no, you will get him something else he wants later. Tell or show him what else he might get (e.g., access to his games or toys later on).

TRY REWARD OR LOSS SYSTEMS

+ **Part of the skill of "accepting no" is the idea that children will get something else they wanted for accepting no.** These rewards can be privileges they normally get as part of their regular routine. However, one can also use a point system for special rewards, giving points every time children accept no or do not ask for something. Those points can be exchanged at the end of the week for rewards like a new toy, game, or special trip.

+ **When tantrums occur after children are denied what they want,** the behavior can be ignored, or one might use a consequence of not taking the children out again where they had the tantrum. Although one could use a distraction to diffuse the meltdown, one should avoid giving the child what they had wanted, as this will only increase the likelihood of more tantrums in the future.

CONSIDER BIOLOGICAL AND PHYSICAL STRATEGIES

+ **As stated before, vigorous exercise can improve mood and self-control,** and thus may temporarily increase willingness to accept no.

+ **When the above interventions have failed,** and difficulty with impulse control exists across many situations, severely limiting the child's ability to function at home or in school, then medication may be a consideration in conjunction with a thorough evaluation by a mental health professional.

Okay, Time to Stop Playing

"Turn off the TV and come to dinner." "Recess is over, let's get back to work." "I said turn the computer off and let's do your homework." "No more play time outside; come in and take your bath." These are all common situations in which we ask children to stop doing something fun to do something less enjoyable. This is a hard transition for most children to make. It was certainly difficult for Tim.

Tim was a twelve-year-old who was obsessed with his video games. He refused to stop playing the games at home when his parents asked him to come to dinner, do homework, or to go to bed. When told to stop, he would stall, saying, "One more minute," and then scream at his parents if they continued to tell him to stop. If they took the video game from him he would scream louder, saying, "I hate you!" and begin to cry. His upset could last an hour unless he became occupied with something else.

His parents had tried to limit access to the video games during the week to avoid these difficulties. Tim would then find something else to do, such as watch TV, build models, or play outside. The problem was that he would become equally unwilling to stop these other activities.

CHANGE THE TRIGGERS

To begin with, we created a schedule for playtime with a clear stopping time that was non-negotiable. After his homework was completed he could play until 6:30 p.m., which was dinnertime. After dinner, he could play for another thirty minutes. His parents used a timer and a written schedule so there would be no surprises for Tim.

We also eased the transition from fun to less enjoyable things by first asking him to do easier things when having to stop an activity. For example, when he was asked to turn off a game and come to dinner, his parents first asked him to come decorate his dinner plate (he liked to arrange the food on his plate). This was an easier first task than asking him to come and sit still at the dinner table. Similarly, for bedtime, the first thing they asked him to do was to pick out what books he wanted to read (rather than asking him to do something less fun for him, such as brushing his teeth).

TEACH SKILLS TO DEAL WITH THE TRIGGERS

We taught Tim that if he could stop playing at the designated time, his parents would trust him and let him play again later. For example, stopping before dinner allowed him to play for thirty minutes after dinner. Stopping after the thirty-minute post-dinner period would allow him to play again the next day after school. He was learning that stopping was not forever, and stopping on time ensured that he could get back to it again later.

We used a visual aid for this skill, showing him stick-figure drawings on index cards depicting how, if he stopped playing his video game, his parents would be proud and let him get back to it later. His parents went over the stick-figure drawings just prior to letting Tim play the video game in order to prepare him before he got too involved with it. Sometimes, seeing the payoff for stopping on time is better than just hearing the words, especially for children who may not always attend to what their parents are saying.

TRY REWARD OR LOSS SYSTEMS

In addition to the natural reward of getting to go back to an activity later if Tim stopped on time, his parents also set up a point system. Every time Tim stopped an activity when asked, he received a point. Points could later be exchanged for long-term rewards, such as buying a new game or having a special privilege on the weekend. This was a concrete way of recognizing Tim's efforts to stop a favored activity on time. If he refused to stop an activity, he lost out on time to do that activity later.

The first two days of the program Tim was inconsistent with keeping to the schedule. After seeing that he did get what he wanted when he stopped on time, he began to accept the routine. Moreover, with increased awareness of the importance of stopping on time, he was able to perform this skill in places beyond home, such as school and family trips.

Quick Reference Guide for Problems Stopping a Fun Activity

CHANGE THE TRIGGERS

+ **Sensory stimulation.** Sometimes children are so engaged in an activity it is hard to get their attention. Computer games and TV can provide so much stimulation that children cannot even hear an adult ask them to stop. It may be necessary to get into children's line of vision to get their attention. Then, with advance warning, turn off the TV or computer.

+ **Timing of the situation.** Children will have greater ability to stop an activity when there is a natural end to it. For instance, if they are outside playing a game, try to direct them to come inside when the game is over. Or if they are watching a show, time the directive to stop when the show is over or there is a commercial.

+ **Task difficulty**

  – *Before they begin the activity, schedule the time* when they will have to stop.

  – *Remind them ahead of time* that if they stop on time they will be able to go back to the activity at a later time.

  – *Give warnings* that the time to stop is coming up and use a timer.

  – *Make it easier to stop an activity by scheduling another fun activity.* For example, at home it will be easier to stop playing outside if they can come in to play a quick game at the table before dinnertime. In school it is easier to come back from recess if they can engage in a fun activity in class before doing more challenging work.

+ **Visual supports**

  – *Use a visual schedule* showing when they must stop an activity and when they can resume it.

– Use a *visual timer* (digital or color-coded timer) to help children know when they will have to stop.

TEACH SKILLS TO DEAL WITH THE TRIGGERS

Explain the hidden payoff of stopping a fun activity: "Others will trust you to do the activity again later." To practice stopping something fun:

+ **Begin by playing games that do not interest them too much,** so it will be easier to stop. Then direct them to stop and put away the game, praising them for doing so. Explain how much you trust them now and are willing to let them play again because you see that they can stop on time.

+ **Remind them of the skill** moments before they begin fun activities. Tell them that if they stop at the designated time, you will trust them to do the activity again later.

TRY REWARD OR LOSS SYSTEMS

+ **Besides the natural rewards of getting to resume a favored activity, you can use a point system.** Points can be given every time the child stops an activity when told. Those points can be exchanged at the end of the week for material rewards or special privileges.

+ **When tantrums occur after being told to stop an activity,** you can limit access to that activity for some period of time. Explain to children that they cannot be trusted to start an activity if they cannot stop the activity on time.

CONSIDER BIOLOGICAL AND PHYSICAL STRATEGIES

+ **These strategies resemble those of the previous situations related to waiting.** Vigorous exercise has been shown to improve mood and self-control, and thus may increase a child's willingness to stop a favored activity when told.

+ **When the above interventions have failed,** and difficulty with impulse control exists across many situations, severely limiting the child's ability to function at home or in school, then consultation with a mental health professional would be wise and medication may be a consideration.

9

THREATS
TO SELF-IMAGE

MOM, OUR TEAM LOST THE FOOTBALL GAME AT RECESS AGAIN... BUT AT LEAST MY STOCK PORTFOLIO IS UP ANOTHER 145% THIS YEAR. I THINK I WILL BUY MY OWN NFL TEAM.

Meltdowns often occur when children believe troublesome situations result from personal inadequacy. For example, dealing with losing and making mistakes lead to greater frustration if the child attributes these situations to his or her lack of ability. Similarly, being teased will lead to greater frustration when the child believes the negative remarks others say. All these situations are easier to handle when children do not believe negative information about themselves. Instead, they might see losing or making mistakes as something to do with the challenging situation, rather than with their own abilities. They might see teasing as a reflection of problems the teaser has, rather than a deficit within themselves.

Winning Isn't Everything

Shawn was an eight-year-old third-grader who was a terrific reader, did well academically, yet struggled with competitive games despite his interest in them. Shawn could not tolerate losing any games at home or in school. Whether he was playing sports, a board game, or an academic game in class, Shawn cried when he lost, calling himself a "loser," and at times throwing the game pieces or balls at others around him. In addition, he yelled at his teammates if he was on a losing team in gym or in the classroom.

No amount of consoling seemed to help Shawn when he was in the throes of his upset. The only thing that seemed to work was if he played again and won. Many other students, as well as his sister and parents, did not want to play with him because they knew how upset he got.

CHANGE THE TRIGGERS

After consulting with the parents, we decided to sign Shawn up for activities in which he was less likely to have problems with losing—either because the activities were not competitive, or because he was already very good at them. We signed him up for swim lessons in which he did not have to race others, and encouraged his participation in chess tournaments, as he was quite gifted in this area.

We arranged with the school to help steer him away from more competitive recess activities and, instead, to have him play on the jungle gym. However, sports during gym time continued to be a challenge, as he initially continued to cry or get angry at his teammates when his team lost.

110

TEACH SKILLS TO DEAL WITH THE TRIGGERS

We taught Shawn that there were always two games he was playing, the particular sport or board game, and the invisible "friendship" game. If he lost the sport game and did not get angry, he could win a friend and others would play with him again. We convinced him that maintaining self-control and winning friends were far more important than winning games.

We also explained that losing a game did not mean that he was not smart or talented. We went over his strengths and talents and explained that the outcome of games is not always a reflection of these abilities, but is rather due to a combination of luck and effort.

The key to being able to use these skills was to ensure that his parents and teachers reminded him of the importance of the invisible game before he began to play anything. They did not wait until he lost to go over this, because by then he would already be too upset to listen.

TRY REWARD OR LOSS SYSTEMS

We backed up the importance of self-control and friendship by creating a home point system that earned Shawn rewards (e.g., buying a new game, book, video or toy) for maintaining control if he lost a game. In fact, if Shawn won a game he received one point, but if he lost a game and did not get mad, he would get two points. In other words, Shawn got more points for losing without getting mad than he did for winning a game. For kids like Shawn, this rarely leads to a desire to lose, but rather decreases the importance of winning.

We had the school create a similar reward chart for gym. If Shawn lost a game and did not get angry, he got two points. If he won, he got one point, and if he lost and got angry, he received no points. Points went home to be added to his point system, where they could be exchanged for rewards.

After two weeks of earning praise and rewards for handling losing, Shawn's self-esteem grew, and he commented on how much better he was at controlling himself. With this newfound confidence, he was soon able to tolerate losing graciously without any rewards.

Quick Reference Guide
for Problems Dealing with Losing

CHANGE THE TRIGGERS

+ **Sensory stimulation.** Many competitive situations have overwhelming sensory stimulation that contributes to children's difficulties coping with losing. Recess and gym time often are noisy, hot, involve lots of physical contact, and constant movement by peers. In this chaotic environment, losing a game may be one stressor too many. It might be necessary to reduce the level of stimulation to increase the frustration tolerance of a student:

  – Consider playing games in a quieter area with fewer children.

  – Consider surrounding the child with less competitive, more cooperative peers.

+ **Timing of the situation.** Students may be more able to tolerate losing when they have just experienced success in another area. If they are already frustrated by some other task, it is not wise to have them engage in competitive activities.

+ **Task difficulty**

  – *Select games at which they can excel.* Know your child's strengths. Not all students have to be jocks; there are plenty of non-athletic games that students can play, such as board games, treasure hunts, follow the leader, charades, twenty questions, and other guessing games.

  – *Select non-competitive games.* Some children enjoy engaging in pretend or exploratory games, like digging for worms, collecting rocks, pretending to fight pirates, or running from dinosaurs.

  – *Emphasize the value of sportsmanship* over winning. Before playing games, parents and teachers can prime children to

112

value sportsmanship rather than winning. Trophies can be awarded for getting along rather than winning.

+ **Visual supports.** Post a visual reminder of the skill "dealing with losing" in the game area. This might be words or pictures indicating how losing a game without getting angry helps to win friends. (See Baker, 2001 & 2003).

TEACH SKILLS TO DEAL WITH THE TRIGGERS

Explain that one is always playing two games, a competitive game and the *"invisible game" of friendship and self-control.* If you lose a game and do not get angry, you win the invisible game. Success in life often depends much more on self-control and friendship than on winning competitive games.

+ **Review activities in which the child excels.** Explain that no one can be great at every activity every time. Remind the child that for each game he might lose, he has performed well at another time.

+ **Remind the child just before competitive games** about the importance of winning the "invisible game" of self-control and friendship. Explain that you are more interested in whether he can stay calm than whether he wins a sport or board game.

TRY REWARD OR LOSS SYSTEMS

+ **Reward children for maintaining control** when they lose a game. Point systems can be used in which they get greater points for losing a game and remaining calm than for winning a game. Points can be exchanged for material rewards or special privileges.

+ **If tantrums occur after losing, it is best to avoid using punishments.** If, however, the child has hurt others or made a mess, he should apologize and clean up.

It's Okay To Make Mistakes

Maya was a thirteen-year-old girl with some mild learning difficulties that affected her reading comprehension and math skills. She had always been hard on herself, yet she had performed well enough in elementary school that she did not receive any special help. Since her transition to middle school, Maya's frustration with work had intensified. When she made a mistake, she would grumble, bite her hands and pick at herself—often until she bled. She had marks on her hands from biting, and scabs on her arms and legs from digging into her skin.

She continued to do well academically, despite her frustrations. However, this made the school hesitant to provide her with academic supports. She openly admitted that she could not stand making mistakes. She feared that any mistake would lead to bad grades and eventually prevent her from getting into college. At home, she would rip up her homework if she made the slightest error, making her parents reluctant to give her any feedback about her work. When playing games with peers she had similar problems, biting at her skin and sometimes walking off angrily if she made a mistake. This made it difficult for her to make new friends, although she had retained one close friend since preschool.

CHANGE THE TRIGGERS

Despite Maya's academic success, the parents and I convinced the school that her frustration level signaled the need for more academic support. She was able to receive a support class that helped her prepare for the reading content in different classes so that she was less likely to make errors in reading comprehension. She was also given help with math and extra time on tests to check over her work.

At home, in order to reduce the likelihood of mistakes, I had her parents review with Maya how to approach her homework before she attempted it, rather than just reviewing her work after she was finished.

TEACH SKILLS TO DEAL WITH THE TRIGGERS AND TRY REWARD OR LOSS SYSTEMS

After consulting with her parents and a counselor in school, we all worked with Maya on how to help her interpret her mistakes. We explained that she was not supposed to do everything right, otherwise she would not need to be in school and that other kids also made mistakes even if they did not say so. We further explained that it is only through mistakes that people learn. When we get something right, we rarely focus on it, but when we make a mistake, it forces us to think about what we are doing so we can learn more. We emphasized that the more mistakes we make, the more we can learn, but that fear of making mistakes can stop us from learning.

Then I had her parents request that she make a mistake each day so she could learn something. They told her they would give her two points every time she made a mistake and did not get angry, and one point for just doing her work without making mistakes. We asked that her math and language arts teacher also report to them when she handled a mistake well, so she could receive her points.

Although points could be exchanged for rewards and privileges, Maya never asked for any material rewards. She was satisfied with the ample praise she received from her teachers and parents for handling mistakes with less upset.

Maya continued in counseling to help her reduce her self-imposed pressure to succeed and allay her worries about getting into college (she was only in middle school). With the focused work on dealing with mistakes, and continued help in reducing her perfectionism and worries about the future, Maya stopped biting and picking at herself and generally seemed to be a happier person. She even made another good friend.

Quick Reference Guide for Problems Dealing with Mistakes

CHANGE THE TRIGGERS

+ **Sensory stimulation.** Children are much more likely to make errors when there is too much competing stimulation while they are working. It is important to have a quieter area to work in, where there will be less disruption from others:

  – Consider creating a distraction-free area by using cardboard to make cubicle-like workspaces in class or at home.

  – Some students may find a "white noise" machine helpful to drown out distracting noises.

  – Some students find the flicker of fluorescent lighting to be distracting and perform better with incandescent lighting.

+ **Timing of the situation.** Difficult tasks should not be attempted when the child is overly tired or hungry, because she will be more likely to make errors.

+ **Task difficulty**

  – *Pre-teach difficult work* so that the child is less likely to make mistakes during class. For example, children can go over class lessons, review book chapters, or math concepts before they are asked to participate in class.

  – *Do not mark or correct work.* If children make a mistake, do not point it out; just go over the concepts with which they need more help. As they gain confidence, it will be possible to slowly begin to start correcting their work again.

  – *Have children check over their own work* before handing it in.

  – *Break down larger assignments* into smaller increments and ask the child to just do a smaller part of it.

- Change recall tasks into *multiple-choice* tasks. For example, in a history class, instead of asking a child to recall why a particular war began, provide several possible answers and ask her to select the right one.

+ **Visual supports to avoid making errors**

- *Use graphic organizers.* These are visual maps that summarize information in a web format to aid in comprehension and later recall. For example, a child might be helped to summarize the main points of a story and show with arrows how different ideas are connected. The web can be used to aid in understanding how the ideas relate to each other and help her recall the information later to write or talk about the topic. (See sample below.)

My School Trip

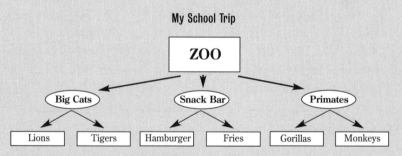

- *Use a cue card or poster* to summarize the steps needed to perform a particular task, such as doing a math problem or writing task, rather than relying on verbal instructions alone.

- Ask the child to *repeat written instructions* before engaging in the task, to learn what she did or did not understand.

TEACH SKILLS TO DEAL WITH THE TRIGGERS

+ **Explain that it is okay to make mistakes; that is how we learn.** No one gets everything right—otherwise there would be nothing to learn.

+ **Try to learn from your mistake by asking for help and try-ing again.**

+ **The sooner you correct a mistake, the sooner you will be done.** Some children do not like correcting their work because it keeps them from playtime. They need to understand that it takes less time to correct the work than to argue about it.

+ **Model and role-play the skill** by purposefully making mis-takes with simple activities such as spelling a word or solving a math problem.

TRY REWARD OR LOSS SYSTEMS

+ **Reward children for maintaining control** when they make a mistake. Point systems can be used in which students get *more* points for making a mistake and remaining calm than they do for getting their work done without mistakes. This helps them value dealing with mistakes more than trying to be perfect. Points can be exchanged for material rewards or special privileges.

+ **Avoid using punishment** with children who are already frus-trated with themselves.

CONSIDER BIOLOGICAL AND PHYSICAL STRATEGIES

+ **Students are more likely to make mistakes when they have attention problems.** Some supplements (e.g., omega-3 fatty acids) and certain medications can be effective in improving attention in children with ADHD. In addition, persistent perfec-tionism can be a sign of a more pervasive anxiety problem, and certain medications can greatly reduce anxiety. However, medica-tions always carry the risk of side effects, thus the decision to medicate should be made only when other strategies have failed and only after a thorough consultation with a physician.

But Names Will Never Hurt You

Mike was an intelligent, eleven-year-old boy. Although he excelled academically, he was not athletically inclined, avoided most physical activity and had become overweight. In addition, he tended to monopolize conversations by discussing his passion, old movies. Often he would continue to tell movie plots well beyond his peers' willingness to listen.

Mike had no true friends at school and generally sat by himself at lunch. Like many boys in middle school who do not excel athletically and whose interests do not overlap with others', Mike was teased. Middle school is often a time when students make the transition from dependence on their parents to greater reliance on their peer group. In an effort to belong, peers often try hard to conform and adopt the interests and values of others, harshly rejecting those who are different. Mike was certainly different and, unfortunately, a scapegoat for some of his peers. Many boys taunted him mercilessly, calling him a nerd, gay, and "movie freak," bumping into him in the hallway, and refusing to work with him in class.

Although teasing was not new to Mike, it had certainly worsened when he entered middle school. He began to refuse to go to school, creating power struggles at home that led to meltdowns from his parents as well as from Mike.

When his parents requested that the school address the teasing problem, the administration responded by suggesting that Mike receive counseling to help him deal with these stressors. Although counseling might help him to deal better with the teasing, it was not going to stop him from being teased.

In fact, Mike had seen a counselor in school on several occasions. They had discussed how he could respond to the teasing, but he complained that no strategy worked. The kids continued to tease him. From my point of view, the school's approach was shortsighted. It was not Mike's job to stop the teasing. That was the job of the school staff, who, thus far, had not protected him. Mike's job was simply to be able to report when he was bullied and to get to a point where these events no longer had the power to hurt his self-esteem.

CHANGE THE TRIGGERS

The most important way to address Mike's problem was to try to stop the constant barrage of teasing. I supported the parents in their efforts to get the school to do two things:

+ Confront and monitor the accused bullies.

+ Create a peer leader program to surround Mike with students willing to stand up for him and others, and engage him socially at lunch and other unstructured times.

At our urging, the school staff spoke to the accused teasers to let them know that they were being monitored because students had reported that they had been teasing others. Mike's name was not mentioned to them. So that Mike or any other student could feel safe reporting bullying, we did not reveal the names of those reporting these incidents. The teasers were warned that there would be detention if they continued. More importantly, with their parents' approval, they were provided with conflict management and empathy training in several sessions with a guidance counselor. These lessons stressed tolerance and understanding others' feelings.

With help from the guidance counselors, we selected potential "peer leaders" who were asked to facilitate social interaction for students who were often isolated at lunch and other unstructured times. Consent forms went home to their parents. Then, during a lunch period, they were provided with training to be "peer leaders." They were asked to participate once a week in a "lunch bunch" group at the guidance center, where they could interact with other students who might "be shy or need some help in making more friends." Similarly, they were asked to help stand up for these more isolated students during the school day by telling would-be bullies to stop, or going to get help from a teacher if they witnessed any bullying behavior. (See Baker 2003 & 2006, in which I discuss setting up peer buddy programs in more detail).

Individual counseling sessions also continued so that Mike had a regular opportunity to report any ongoing bullying issues, and to continue to work on ways to handle teasing. In addition, the counselor helped Mike become more aware of his conversational style so that he would not obsess over movies with those who were not interested in this topic.

TEACH SKILLS TO DEAL WITH THE TRIGGERS

In Mike's individual sessions, he and his counselor worked on how to deal with teasing. The following steps were taught:

1. Ask if the person was serious or just kidding.
2. Consider that the person who teases has the problem, not you.
3. Calmly tell the person to stop.
4. If the person continues, walk away.
5. If the person still teases or threatens harm, tell an adult.

The first two steps involved helping Mike to protect his self-esteem. He discovered that when others teased, it did not mean that there was something "bad" about him. Sometimes teasers just wanted to play (e.g., when their comments were not about sensitive issues and they were trying to get Mike to laugh). Other times, teasers intended to hurt fellow students as a result of their own problems. He learned that bullies often feel powerless in their lives and thus try to use teasing to exert power over others.

Next, Mike practiced remaining calm when responding to teasing so as not to satisfy those who might want him to get upset. Most importantly, he was taught the importance of reporting bullying as an essential step in putting a stop to it. Initially reluctant to "tattle," Mike learned the difference between playful teasing and chronic verbal abuse, and the need to report the latter.

TRY REWARD OR LOSS SYSTEMS

The only rewards used here were the natural effects of the intervention: that teasing virtually stopped, other than an occasional playful comment.

Mike and his parents reported a remarkable positive change in his attitude towards school. He now looked forward to going to school to be with friends. He participated along with other previously isolated students in the lunch bunch group surrounded by peer leaders. For the most part, the peer leaders provided Mike with a friendly environment, protected him from bullying in and outside the group, but did not become "true" friends outside of school. However, some of the other more isolated students who had also joined the lunch bunch group found that they had many common interests with Mike. As a result, Mike developed one very close friend with whom he got together outside of school.

By protecting Mike from bullying and creating opportunities for friendship, Mike's experience in school dramatically improved. His parents felt that he was indeed a much happier child.

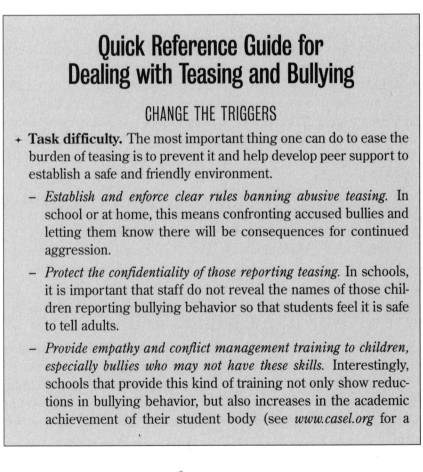

Quick Reference Guide for Dealing with Teasing and Bullying

CHANGE THE TRIGGERS

+ **Task difficulty.** The most important thing one can do to ease the burden of teasing is to prevent it and help develop peer support to establish a safe and friendly environment.

  – *Establish and enforce clear rules banning abusive teasing.* In school or at home, this means confronting accused bullies and letting them know there will be consequences for continued aggression.

  – *Protect the confidentiality of those reporting teasing.* In schools, it is important that staff do not reveal the names of those children reporting bullying behavior so that students feel it is safe to tell adults.

  – *Provide empathy and conflict management training to children, especially bullies who may not have these skills.* Interestingly, schools that provide this kind of training not only show reductions in bullying behavior, but also increases in the academic achievement of their student body (see *www.casel.org* for a review of the research on these programs). At home, parents need to teach ways for siblings to manage their conflicts without insults.

- *Create a peer buddy program for children who are isolated.* This involves sensitizing peers to the needs of isolated children and training them to engage with and protect these students. Examples of peer sensitivity programs can be found in my social skill manuals (Baker, 2003 & 2005).

- *Provide ongoing counseling to children* who have been chronically teased in order to check whether the teasing continues and to teach ways to handle peer problems.

+ **Visual supports.** *Use a cue card or checklist* to summarize how to resolve conflicts and respond to teasing (see skill steps below).

TEACH SKILLS TO DEAL WITH THE TRIGGERS

+ **Make sure the child is not doing things that provoke others.** If being bossy or rude to others contributes to your child being teased, then your child must first learn to stop provoking others. You will need to explain to your youngster what kinds of words and actions might bother others.

+ **Dealing with teasing.** The main thrust here is to help the child maintain self-esteem and not let the teasing control how he or she feels. The steps for dealing with teasing are outlined below. The first two steps emphasize that what the teaser says is not necessarily true, thus taking some of the power out of the words.

1. Ask if the person was serious or just kidding.
2. Consider that the person who teases has the problem, not you.
3. Calmly tell the person to stop.
4. If the person continues, walk away.
5. If the person still teases or threatens harm, tell an adult.

+ **Managing conflicts by talking it out.** This skill is best suited for situations in which a close friend or family member said or did something that upset the child. Presumably, close friends and family care about his feelings, so it is wise to tell them how he feels. This is not the skill to use with a bully who may not care about his feelings. When it comes to strangers or bullies, it is best to use the skill "dealing with teasing" outlined above.

1. Schedule a time to talk. Sometimes others are not ready to discuss a problem when you are.

2. Tell the other person what you want without insulting him. Use an "I am statement":

   "I FEEL _____ (feeling word)

   WHEN YOU _____ (what they did or said)

   BECAUSE _____. (the reason it upset you)

   WHAT I WANT OR NEED IS _____."

3. Listen to the other person's side so you can offer solutions that work for both of you.

TRY REWARD OR LOSS SYSTEMS

+ **Depending on the nature of the teasing problem, we may want to reward children for different skills.** Consider which of these behaviors you want to reward.

  – Handling teasing peacefully without seeking revenge

  – Not provoking others

  – Standing up for others who are teased

+ **Children can also be rewarded as a group for handling conflicts peacefully.** For example, families can create a "kindness jar" so that any time siblings resolve a conflict calmly, parents can put a marble in a jar. When they have enough marbles, the siblings or groups of children can be rewarded with a special outing or celebration.

+ **Children who tease others after being warned to stop repeatedly may need to lose a privilege.**

10

UNMET WISHES FOR ATTENTION

Many a meltdown has occurred when a child has been denied attention from a parent, another adult, or a peer. In this chapter, we examine three common situations that involve unmet wishes for attention:

1. When a child wants to play, but the other person does not.

2. When there is competition for adult attention, as when siblings argue over who got more.

3. Going to bed at night. This is the most complicated because it involves the desire for parental attention, fear of separation, and

having to end playtime, all of which can converge to create major upsets.

Children who have trouble waiting in general will also have trouble waiting for adult attention and thus some of the strategies in Chapter 8 will be applicable here as well. However, the need for attention can occur in children who otherwise do not have trouble waiting. Getting parental attention, or being able to manage at times without it, requires more than the ability to wait.

I Can't Play With You Now

When I was younger, I used to love watching the Pink Panther movies starring Peter Sellers as the bumbling Inspector Clouseau. Whenever Clouseau entered his home, he had to be ready for the surprise karate attacks by his sidekick, Kato. Clouseau had instructed Kato to engage in these impromptu assaults to keep the inspector fit and ready for anything.

Without much warning, when my son turned six years old, he became Kato. After a long, hard day of work, I would walk through my front door to a seemingly quiet home, until, out of nowhere, my son would jump on me from behind, wrestle me to the ground and sit on my head. My directives to wait until I could put my briefcase down and change out of my work clothes were seldom heeded.

His desire to wrestle and my desire to relax led to a recurrent power struggle. If he continued to pull and grab at me despite my warnings, I would put him in time out. However, the next night we would be right back at it. One night I was particularly tired and in no mood for play. I walked in, warned him not to attack me, as I had to take care of some paper work. He grabbed me anyway, smiling as he tried to pull me down to the ground. I tried to put him in time out, but he resisted. I threatened to take his favorite toys if he did not go to time out. After a fair amount of crying and screaming, he went to time out for five minutes. Afterward, both of us exhausted, he said, "You know, Dad, I was only trying to play with you. I hardly get to see you when you work so much."

126

I realized he was absolutely right. He had continued to try to engage me in play, just not in the right way. Although I did not like the "Kato" routine, he deserved to have more playtime with me.

CHANGE THE TRIGGERS

My son and I agreed that after I put away my briefcase and changed my clothes, I would play with him as soon as I got home. To accomplish this, I made sure I finished what I needed to do before getting home, even if this meant arriving twenty minutes later. We agreed upon several activities we both enjoyed. This even included some wrestling, as long as we both agreed to play-fight rather than engage in the surprise "Kato" attacks.

TEACH SKILLS TO DEAL WITH THE TRIGGERS

I explained to my son that I would play with him if he asked nicely, and was willing to wait until I was ready. When I arrived home I would prompt him to ask, and then wait for the designated time. As he became reassured that I would indeed play, his ability to wait increased.

TRY REWARD OR LOSS SYSTEMS

The natural reward for asking and waiting to play was that he got to play with me. If, on the other hand, he went back to the surprise attacks, I had him wait an additional ten minutes longer to play with me.

Overall, we were both more satisfied and looked forward to our playtime together. Several years after this Kato period, my son and I still play at least one game each night. Fortunately for both of us, we have moved on to games like Uno, Chess, Scrabble, and other calm activities before bedtime.

Quick Reference Guide for Problems When No One Wants to Play

CHANGE THE TRIGGERS

+ **Sensory stimulation.** Many children who constantly want attention generally have a need for more stimulation. They get bored quickly and do not always know how to entertain themselves. Thus it is crucial that these children have engaging activities to do while waiting to play with others. Examples might include:

  – A "to do" box that has several activities from which to choose

  – Access to favored games or activities, such as books, puzzles, or handheld video games to help them pass the time while waiting

  – Helping their parents with a job, such as getting groceries, making dinner, or setting the table

+ **Timing of the situation.** Create regularly scheduled times to play so that children do not have to keep asking. In addition, parents may want to finish their work before being around their children so that they can be fully available to their kids.

+ **Task difficulty**

  – *When possible, reduce the wait time to get others attention.*

  – *Have children help those from whom they want attention:* For example, children can help their parents complete chores so they can get to playtime more quickly.

  – *Pair children with peer buddies:* In schools, we can create peer buddy programs so that students always have someone to play with. This involves sensitizing peers to the needs of isolated children and training them to engage these students. Examples of peer sensitivity programs can be found in my social skill manuals (Baker, 2003 & 2005).

128

+ **Visual supports.** *Use a cue card or checklist* to remind children how to ask others to play and when others will be available.

TEACH SKILLS TO DEAL WITH THE TRIGGERS

Teach how to ask and wait to play. Sometimes children forget to ask to play, and instead engage in self-defeating, irritating behaviors to try to engage others. Remind children of the following steps to successfully get others to play:

1. Choose people and peers who like to play with you. Avoid those who usually say no.

2. Ask the person to play.

3. If they are not ready, ask when they can play.

4. Find another activity to do while you are waiting for others to play with you.

5. Choose activities that you both like.

TRY REWARD OR LOSS SYSTEMS

+ **Children can be rewarded for asking nicely to play and waiting patiently.** The best reward is to spend time playing with the children. One can also use a point system for asking nicely and waiting. Points can build up to purchase long-term rewards such as new toys, games, or special privileges.

+ **If children try to get attention in irritating ways or do not wait despite your reminders, the natural consequence would be to delay when they can play.** For example, every time they try to get your attention after you asked them to wait, you can add additional minutes of waiting time before play.

Don't Be Jealous

Sibling rivalry has many faces. Kids argue to see who is faster, stronger or smarter as they carve out their own separate identities. They fight over access to toys, food, and all resources in the house. Perhaps the most valuable resource for which they compete is parental attention.

Laura was a seven-year-old girl living with an eight-year-old brother, Michael. Like many siblings, they had a love/hate relationship. They were the best of pals when conspiring against their parents to sneak candy or stay outside and play after they were told to come in. Yet they also argued over things like access to the TV remote and who would get the last cookie. Laura especially seemed to have trouble tolerating situations in which her brother got special attention from her parents.

On the weekends, Laura's dad coached Michael's soccer team. When the family would go to watch the games, Laura would hold onto her Dad continuously, interfering with his ability to coach. If Mom tried to engage her in another activity or stay at home with her, Laura would scream and tantrum.

Similarly, if Mom or Dad sat next to Michael at a movie or at the dinner table, Laura got in between so she could be closer to her parents. If Michael tried to re-establish his position, Laura would cry intensely and start to kick her brother, who would initially retaliate and then succumb to her tantrum to stop the misery.

Whenever Michael got a snack from the refrigerator, a goodie bag at a birthday party, new clothes for school, or any other item, Laura wanted to make sure she got hers. "How come Michael got something?" she would complain. "That's not fair!" Reminding her that she just got something days earlier did not satisfy her. Often it was impossible in the moment to give her something of equal value in her eyes, and she would continue to fuss and cry. Her parents tried ignoring her, but she would continue to harass them. After about twenty minutes, they would begin to take away toys or privileges. This only seemed to inflame her sense of injustice. This had become a repetitive problem that her parents could no longer ignore or tolerate.

CHANGE THE TRIGGERS

Although the ultimate goal was to help Laura tolerate periods in which she was not getting exactly the same attention or gifts as her brother, with my help the parents recognized that they could avoid some of the problems by careful planning of how they attended to their children. First, whenever buying items for one child, they tried to get something for both. Second, they regularly scheduled exclusive time for Laura with her parents, especially when Michael had a special event with his parents (e.g., at his soccer matches). I suggested that they refer to this as "Laura's Special Time" to highlight that she was getting extra attention from her parents. They would play Laura's favorite games, schedule a play date for her, or take her out to the mall or movies while Michael had a play date or soccer match.

For the dinner table and when going out to the movies, I helped the family make a chart of whose turn it was to sit between her parents. With preparation and the chart, Laura began to tolerate when Michael got the preferred seat. We also created a chart to keep track of when Laura and Michael received items such as clothes or gifts. Reviewing the chart helped Laura to see that Michael really did not get more than her over time.

TEACH SKILLS TO DEAL WITH THE TRIGGERS

Using a quote from Rick Lavoie, a famous learning disabilities consultant, we taught Laura that "fairness is not equal … Fairness means that every student receives what he needs" (Lavoie, 1989). A great story to help children understand this concept was provided to me by a teacher in Bayonne New Jersey. She said:

> "Imagine a student comes back from recess to tell his teacher that he cut his finger. The teacher says, let me wash your finger and put a bandage on it. Then another child comes back to class complaining that his stomach hurts, so the teacher says, let me wash your finger and put a bandage on it. Then another child skips happily back to class without any complaints, and the teacher says, let me wash your finger and put a bandage on it." (Pat Berezny, personal communication, 2004).

We asked Laura, "What's wrong with this story?" She began to understand that equal is not always fair. We helped her to understand that she and Michael need different things at different times. Although they would not always get the same things, they would get what they needed. We explained, "Sometimes Michael gets clothes for school when he grows out of them and you won't. And you might get new shoes when you grow out of them and Michael won't. Sometimes Michael will have a soccer match that we will watch, and sometimes you will go for a walk with us when Michael can't." In essence, we helped Laura understand that, in the end, her parents would do everything they could to make sure she would get what she needed.

TRY REWARD OR LOSS SYSTEMS

Laura was rewarded with ample praise and the promise of receiving her own "special time" with her parents for tolerating when Michael received attention. If, instead, she continued to fuss and demand her parent's immediate attention, they ignored her. If she made that impossible, for example, by grabbing at them or physically pushing her brother aside in order to be close to her parents, they would explain that, since she demanded their attention now, this would cut into her special time later with them.

Fortunately, once she trusted that she would get special time with them, Laura did not persist in demands for her parents' attention. In addition, with the help of the visual charts of when each child received items and got to sit next to their parents, Laura stopped complaining and learned that neither child received more than the other.

Quick Reference Guide
for Jealousy of Others Getting Attention

CHANGE THE TRIGGERS

+ **Sensory stimulation.** Children who require high levels of stimulation in general may demand constant attention and express jealousy when attention is given to others. It is crucial that these children have engaging activities to keep them stimulated when they are not the focus of attention. Examples might include:

  – A "to do" box that has several activities from which to choose

  – Access to favored games or activities, like books, handheld video games or DVD players to help them pass the time while waiting

  – Helping their parents with a job, such as getting groceries, making dinner, or setting the table

+ **Timing of the situation.** Create regularly scheduled "special times" for children to get exclusive attention from an adult. This can be a time to talk, play, or take a special outing. This way, adults can regulate when the attention will come rather than giving in to a child's immediate demands for attention.

+ **Task difficulty**

  – *When buying gifts for one child, try to get something for all the children.* Even birthdays can be a time when all siblings can get a small gift to offset all the attention paid to the birthday child.

  – *When attending to one child, schedule a time to do something special with another child.* For example, if one child has to sit with his parents to work on a special school project, schedule a time to do a project or game with the other children.

  – *Try to turn individual time with one child into group times so everyone gets attention.* When one child needs help with a project, have all the children do a similar project and circulate to help all of them.

– *Have children help each other, rather than rely on adult attention.* For example, if a younger child is learning to ride a bike and an older child is jealous, have the jealous child help teach the younger child how to ride. Offer ample praise for the older child's ability to help the younger one.

+ **Visual supports.** Use a visual schedule to show when each child will get certain kinds of attention so they can see that no one gets more than the other in the long run. Schedules can track who gets alone time with a parent or when children get certain gifts or special treats.

TEACH SKILLS TO DEAL WITH THE TRIGGERS

+ **Explain that fairness does not mean equal treatment.** "Fair" means that everyone gets what he or she needs. This story, as described earlier, can help your child understand this concept.

"Imagine a student comes back from recess to tell his teacher that he cut his finger. The teacher says, let me wash your finger and put a bandage on it. Then another child comes back to class complaining that his stomach hurts, and the teacher says, let me wash your finger and put a bandage on it. Then another child skips happily back to class without any complaints, and the teacher says, let me wash your finger and put a bandage on it." (Pat Berezny, personal communication, 2004).

Ask your child, "What's wrong with this story?" Help her to see that these students have different needs. Treating them exactly the same is silly. Help your child understand that she too will get what she needs.

+ **In the end, everyone will get what they need.** This is essentially the skill of waiting. Using a visual schedule here can be helpful so that children can see what is not always apparent to them: that although they have to wait, eventually they will get the attention they need.

TRY REWARD OR LOSS SYSTEMS

+ **Children should be praised for tolerating when others get attention.** In addition, a special time can be set up each day for a child to receive alone time with a parent or another adult.

+ **When children try to interfere with an adult giving attention to others, such attempts should be ignored.** Sometimes children physically push or grab others so that they cannot be ignored. At these times they can be told that the attention they demand in the moment will cut into their special time later with those adults.

Time to Go to Bed

Robin was a five-year-old girl. Her sister was seven years old. Her parents … well, they felt like they were 100 years old. They had not had much sleep prior to coming to see me, because Robin resisted going to bed and would wake her parents up early each morning. Historically, her parents had established a bedtime routine that was working well enough. One of her parents would read and sing to her until she fell asleep. This routine began to fall apart some time after they had weaned her from her pacifier two months earlier at the urging of their dentist.

At 8:00 p.m. each night, Robin was supposed to brush her teeth, get into her pajamas, and get in bed for story time. As each child had her own room, the parents split up to put each daughter to bed.

When her parents began the routine by saying, "time to brush your teeth," Robin ran away. When cornered, she fought her parents until they could manage to brush her teeth for her. Getting pajamas on was equally challenging. Nothing fit; every outfit was uncomfortable to her and tossed to the floor. After another thirty minutes or so, they managed to get some clothes on. When finally ready to get into bed, she had a burst of energy, jumping up and down, wrestling her parents, and claiming she was not tired. Her parents' efforts to read, tell her a story, or sing to her did not soothe her as she made a litany of demands. "I'm hungry. I want Daddy, no, Mommy. Put the covers on, no, off. I'm thirsty. Can I go in your room?"

After an hour of this, her parents just turned off the light, kissed her good night, and said they would come and check on her in a little bit and then left. She followed them out into their room. They took her back into her room, kissed her, and walked out, promising to check in on her again. She cried and yelled, threatening to wake her sister. Fearful of having both kids awake, the parents decided to stay with her in her room, or sometimes allowed her to fall asleep in their room. The whole bedtime routine lasted over two hours and left her parents irritated and restless when they were finally allowed to sleep.

As if this were not enough, Robin got up early in the morning and demanded that her parents play with her. If they ignored her, she would keep kicking them or jumping on them until they attended to her.

When they shared their story with other families, they were told that they were letting Robin "rule the roost," and that they should be firmer with her at bedtime and in the morning. Some suggested taking away privileges for keeping her parents awake. Others said to try a positive approach and reward her for staying in her room at night and not coming into her parents' room until later in the morning. But promises of rewards and threats of losing privileges proved no match for the anxieties that drove Robin to cling to her parents. No reward or loss was more powerful than the relief Robin had in being near her parents at night and in the morning. To help them address this problem, we needed to better understand the cause of her neediness at night.

Given that the problem had worsened after she had been weaned from her pacifier, we hypothesized that she had lost her primary method of soothing herself at night and needed to learn a way to fall asleep other than relying on her parents. Robin also shared with me and her parents that she was afraid of the dark, heard monsters in her room, and did not want to be alone. Understanding her specific fears and lack of self-soothing skills helped us to design an effective plan.

CHANGE THE TRIGGERS

To address her fear of the dark and monsters, we spoke with Robin about how to make her room less scary at night. We added a brighter nightlight, and equipped her with a flashlight she could keep by her bed in case she thought she saw or heard something. We also explained all the different noises she might hear during the night; how the radiator clanged, the icemaker in the refrigerator clanked, and the floors creaked when Mommy or Daddy went to the bathroom.

In order to help her feel less alone, we loaded her up with her favorite stuffed animals (in addition to the one she always slept with) to keep her company. Then we created a special tape recording of her parents telling her some favorite stories and singing bedtime songs. We had her practice using the tape recorder during the day so she would be quite adept at using the tapes at night.

To help her with early morning rising, we wrote the numeral 7 by her bed, and explained that this must be the first number on her digital clock before she could come into her parents' room. We set up her room with some favored toys and a morning snack so she could take care of herself if she awoke too early.

TEACH SKILLS TO DEAL WITH THE TRIGGERS

The main skill Robin needed to learn was how to soothe herself to sleep. The only way she would learn this was to give her the opportunity to be by herself. We explained that she was never really alone because she always had herself. In fact, we had her record her own voice on the tape saying, "I am never alone because I have my best friend, me." We taught her how to rewind the tape to listen to her bedtime stories, songs, and her own voice as much as she liked.

Then we had her parents go through the bedtime ritual: brushing teeth, pajamas, reading books, and singing a song, and then kissing her goodnight. The plan was to leave her with the tape recorder, remind her that she could hear them on her own, and then promise to come back to check on her shortly. After one minute, they were to return to check in, kiss her and say they would be back in two minutes. After two minutes, they were to return, comfort her briefly and say they would be back in five minutes. They were instructed to continue checking on her until they returned to find her asleep. This strategy of progressive waiting is a variant of the Ferber Method (Ferber, 1985 & 2006), which has been shown to be an effective way to help children fall asleep on their own. Previously, leaving Robin alone even for two minutes would not have worked. They were hopeful that with her tape recorder, flashlight, and stuffed animals, she would make the attempt to self-soothe.

TRY REWARD OR LOSS SYSTEMS

Each night that Robin was able to stay in her own bed until 7:00 a.m. the next morning, she received a sticker. As soon as she got three stickers she could get a new toy. No losses were used for nights she woke her parents up; she just did not earn a sticker.

Robin was anxious but excited to try out her new tape recorder and flashlight. She carefully arranged her stuffed animals around her bed.

Her parents used the Ferber method of progressive waiting, beginning with intervals of one minute, then two, then five. When they tried the first night to push the interval to ten minutes, their daughter cried out for them. So they kept the interval at five minutes the first night. As she trusted they would keep returning, she fell asleep after thirty minutes. This was a great improvement compared to the hours it had taken on other nights.

In the morning, Robin woke up to her favorite toys and a snack. Her parents heard her use the bathroom and go back to her room, where she played by herself as they had instructed the night before. Eventually, her parents came into her room after 7:00 a.m. to hug and kiss her. Her parents offered tremendous praise for her efforts at falling asleep on her own and playing independently in the morning. Robin was clearly proud of her accomplishment, and told every visitor to the house about what she had done.

The next night they used the same routine. With Robin's increased confidence that she could fall asleep without her parents in the room, she was able to tolerate ten-minute intervals before her parents would check on her.

The plan worked well and, after a week, her parents stopped providing stickers and new toys. The only setbacks occurred when they went on vacation and the sleep routine was altered. Upon returning home, they would return to their nightly pattern of checking in on her as she used her tape recorder, flashlight, and stuffed animals and she would resume getting to sleep without her parents in the room.

Quick Reference Guide for Problems with Getting Children to Bed and Letting Parents Sleep

CHANGE THE TRIGGERS

+ **Sensory stimulation**

  – *Create the right conditions for sleep.*
  - Being tired at night depends on having an active day. Early morning exercise and an active day will help increase the probability of sleepiness in the evening.
  - Typically, people sleep better when the room is slightly cooler than it is during the day.
  - Intermittent noise can startle. If it is impossible to reduce the noise level, white-noise machines can be purchased to block intermittent sounds, especially in the morning when traffic, birds, or other noises can wake children too early.
  - Low levels of light are conducive to sleeping; but children's fears of the dark may require the use of nightlights as well as flashlights that can add a sense of security. For early risers, consider the use of room-darkening shades so the sun will not wake them.
  - Provide comfortable bedding that matches the sensory needs of your child (e.g., some like lots of fluffy blankets; others like a firm mattress).

  – *Sensory issues with starting the bedtime ritual*
  - Consider if any part of the bedtime ritual (e.g., brushing teeth or hair, bathing) are irritating. You can start these rituals earlier so they are not associated with bedtime, or you can alter the stimulation (e.g., different flavors of toothpaste, detangling hair with hands rather than a brush).

+ **Timing of the situation.** Create a predictable time to start the bedtime routine. If children are genuinely not tired when their regular bedtime comes, consider waking them up early the next morning to get back to a cycle in which they will be tired by bedtime.

+ **Task difficulty.** To reduce the difficulty of bedtime, *we need to understand the reason for the bedtime problem.* Many children may be in the habit of relying on their parents to comfort them to sleep, not understanding how to soothe themselves. Often the difficulties have to do with fears (of the dark, of monsters, or of being alone), lack of a consistent routine, thinking they are missing something special, or jealousy that another child is getting attention while they sleep.

  - *Create a consistent bedtime routine.* Children are less likely to resist getting ready for bed when the routine is predictable and ends with some pleasurable activity. For example, one could offer the following schedule: "take bath, brush teeth, put on pajamas, play one game with parents, and then get in bed for story time."

  - *Dealing with fear of the dark:* Talk with the child about what kinds of nightlights and flashlights will help him or her feel more secure.

  - *Fear of monsters.* Find out about the noises they hear and sights they see at night that they think are monsters. Explain what the real sources of those noises and sights are (e.g., the radiator, air conditioner, someone walking on squeaky floors). Some parents have also found it helpful to give their children "monster spray" (really water in a spray bottle), pretending that this will keep away all intruders. Be careful using this last tip, as some children may believe that their parents are agreeing that monsters exist.

  - *Fear of being alone.* Give children their favorite stuffed animals to keep them company. Consider making an audiotape or video of you and your children with bedtime stories or songs on it. Allow your children to play these tapes on their own to help them fall asleep.

- *Use Progressive Waiting (the Ferber Method) to help children sleep on their own.* Ferber (1985 & 2006) advocates an approach of leaving children awake after your regular bedtime ritual and then checking on them after progressively longer periods of time until they are asleep. For example, after the usual bedtime ritual, you tell your child you will come back and check on them in one minute. After one minute you return, comfort them, and then say you will check on them in five minutes. Each time period gets increasingly longer, until they have fallen asleep on their own.

- *For nighttime waking.* Walk children back to their room, comfort them briefly but leave them awake with those things that comfort them (e.g., stuffed animal, tape recorder, flashlight) so they can continue to learn to fall asleep on their own. Sometimes parents are too tired to continually put their children back to bed at night. If this is the case, consider putting a sleeping bag in your room for children to sleep in if they come into your room at night. Just remember, whatever you do consistently will end up becoming a habit.

- *Jealousy of other siblings.* If they are jealous that parents will leave them at night and pay attention to other siblings, you can plan to spend a special time with them the next day.

- *Leaving a fun activity to get ready for bed.* Explain to children that if they stop something fun to get ready for bed, they will be able to do something else fun. Try to create one fun activity (playing a game or reading a favored book) after some of the bedtime "chores" (i.e., bathing, brushing teeth, putting on pajamas) so that children will be motivated to cooperate.

+ **Visual supports.** *Use a poster with pictures or words* to show the bedtime routine. Also, help children to read a clock so they will know what time they can wake you. You may have to draw the time next to the clock so they can recognize when morning has come.

TEACH SKILLS TO DEAL WITH THE TRIGGERS

All the strategies described above are meant to make it easier for children to get to bed in a timely way and stay in bed until the morning. These strategies will work better when we can convince our children to want to try them. The following describes the steps to help your child use the strategies above to address their resistance to bedtime:

+ **Help your child understand why bedtime is a problem.** Explore with her if she is afraid (e.g., of the dark, monsters or being alone), jealous of siblings who get to stay up later, or unwilling to stop fun activities.

+ **Have your child collaborate with you to plan ways to solve the problem.** Describe some of the strategies outlined above to reduce fears, allay jealousy, or stop favored activities. Have your child pick the strategies she wants to try. Gaining your child's input will increase motivation to try to implement the plan.

TRY REWARD OR LOSS SYSTEMS

Children can be given stickers that add up to other rewards like toys or special privileges. If getting into bed on time is the issue, then stickers should be given for that. Alternatively, if staying in their own beds is the problem, then stickers can be given for spending the night in their own beds. Most importantly, ample praise should be given for any of these behaviors so children can take pride in their independence. Punishments should be avoided for a child who fears being in her own bed as this may increase anxiety for a child who is already anxious.

CONSIDER BIOLOGICAL AND PHYSICAL STRATEGIES

✦ **Early morning exercise and less active evenings are associated with better sleep patterns.**

✦ **Eating large meals just before bed can interfere with sleep.** Drinking too much liquid can also cause frequent waking to urinate.

✦ **Melatonin may be an effective supplement to aid in sleep** (see Pavonen, Nieminen-VanWendt et al., 2003), but always check with your pediatrician before giving any sleep aid.

11

CLOSING THOUGHTS:
Finding Your Own Way

One of the most important things we parents and professionals can do to avoid meltdowns for ourselves and our children is to have a plan. This book was designed to give you a map to create prevention plans. Although I have outlined fifteen sample plans for you to consider, you will certainly have to design your own to address the specific types of situations that trigger your children's meltdowns.

Chapter 6 provides the template for you to create such plans. A blank "Prevention Plan Form" is provided on the next page for you to use in outlining your prevention plans. As always, the map is not the same as the territory. However, my experience tells me that those who do not give up will find their way. If your children have chronic meltdowns—find the triggers (Chapter 5), change the triggers, and teach them better ways to handle those triggers.

In helping your children, try to appreciate who they are, rather than what you wished them to be. Although we can always teach them new skills, we will have to adjust our expectations to keep in line with who they are at the moment.

Our children will always challenge us. Yet if we can tolerate that discomfort without blaming ourselves or our children, we can avoid our own meltdowns so that we can help our children avoid theirs.

Prevention Plan Form

CHANGE THE TRIGGERS

✦ **Changes to sensory stimulation:**

✦ **Changes to the timing of the situation:**

✦ **Changes to task difficulty:**

✦ **Visual supports used:**

TEACH SKILLS TO DEAL WITH THE TRIGGERS

Triggering Situation	Problem Behavior	Alternative Skills*
Demands, waiting, threats to self-image, unmet wishes for attention		
Other?		

TRY REWARD OR LOSS SYSTEMS

+ **Rewards:**

+ **Losses** (only use if the triggering situation has been modified and the child has been taught a better way to deal with the situation):

CONSIDER BIOLOGICAL AND PHYSICAL STRATEGIES

+ **Dietary changes:**

+ **Exercise, meditation and other physical modes of relaxation:**

+ **Medications** (consider only when other strategies have failed):

REFERENCES

Baker, J. E. (2001). The social skills picture book. Arlington, TX: Future Horizons, Inc.

Baker, J. E. (2003). Social skills training for students with Aspergers syndrome and related social communication disorders. Shawnee Mission, Kansas: Autism Aspergers Publishing Company.

Baker, J. E. (2005). Preparing for life: The complete guide to transitioning to adulthood for those with Autism and Aspergers Syndrome. Arlington, TX: Future Horizons, Inc.

Baker, J. E. (2006). The social skills picture book for high school and beyond. Arlington, TX: Future Horizons, Inc.

Carmichael, M. (2007, March 26). Health for Life: Exercise and the brain. Newsweek, 38-46.

Diener, C. I., & Dweck, C. S. (1978). An analysis of learned helplessness: Continuous changes in performance, strategy, and achievement cognitions following failure. Journal of Personality and Social Psychology, 36. 451-462.

Diener, C. I., & Dweck, C. S. (1980). An analysis of learned helplessness: II. The processing of success. Journal of Personality and Social Psychology, 39. 940-952.

Dweck, C. S. (1975). The role of expectations and attributions in the alleviation of learned helplessness. Journal of Personality and Social Psychology, 31. 674-685.

Faber, A., & Mazlish, E. (2005). How to talk so kids will listen and listen so kids will talk. Collins.

Ferber, R. (1985). Solve your child's sleep problems. Simon & Schuster.

Ferber, R. (2006). Solve your child's sleep problems. Simon & Schuster.

Fermin, M., Hwang, C., Copella, M., & Clark, S. (2004, Summer). Learned Helplessness: The effect of failure on test-taking. Education, v124, n4, p688.

Goleman, D. (1995). Emotional Intelligence. Bantam Books, New York.

Kagan, J. (1994). Galen's Prophecy. New York; Basic Books.

Kingsley, E. P. (1987). Welcome to Holland. Essay posted on the Internet. Copyright Emily Perl Kingsley.

Kranowitz, C. S. (2006). The Out-of-Sync Child: Recognizing and Coping with Sensory Processing Disorder, Revised Edition, Perigee Trade.

Lavoie, R. (1989, January). Developing an educational philosophy: If you don't stand for something, you'll fall for anything. Journal of Learning Disabilities.

Lebow, J. (2007). A look at the evidence: Top 10 research findings of the last 25 years. Psychotherapy Networker, Vol. 31 (2). March/April issue.

Miller, M.C. (2007, March 26). Health for Life: Physical activity and your moods. Newsweek, 48-55.

Oberman, L. M., Hubbard, E. M., McCleery, J. P., Altschuler, E. L., Pineda, J. A., & Ramachandran, V. S. (2005). EEG evidence for mirror neuron dysfunction in autism spectrum disorders. Cognitive Brain Research, Vol. 24, pages 190-198.

Pavonen, E. J., Nieminen-VanWendt, T., et al. (2003). Effectiveness of melatonin in the treatment of sleep disturbances in children with Asperger disorder. Journal of Child and Adolescent Psychopharmacology, 13(1): 83-95.

Sinn, N., Bryan, J., (2007). Effect of supplementation with polyunsaturated fatty acids and micronutrients on ADHD-related problems with attention and behavior. Journal of Developmental & Behavioral Pediatrics, 28(2), 82-91.

Thomas, A., & Chess, S. (1977). Temperament and Development. New York: Brunner/Mazel.